Feed My Heart *God*

By: Sandra Orellana selected

San Miguel de Allende Ministry, Friends, Neighbors & Students

Feed My Heart God

Sandra Orellana

Feed My Heart

© Sandra Orellana 2023

All rights reserved. Without limiting the rights under copyright reserved above, no part of this publication may be reproduced, stored in a retrieval system, or transmitted, in any form or by any means (electronic, mechanical, photocopying, recording or otherwise), without the prior written permission of the copyright owner of this book.

Published by
Lighthouse Christian Publishing
SAN 257-4330
5531 Dufferin Drive
Savage, Minnesota, 55378
United States of America

www.lighthousechristianpublishing.com

God guides us beyond our comfort zone into his purpose
-Sandra Orellana

John 15:16 You did not choose me, but I chose you and appointed you to go and bear fruit – fruit that will last. Then the Father will give you whatever you ask in my name.

Dedication and Gratitude:

To: Jesus for leading me the way to live my life with joy

To: My mother "who" left me recipes

To: Each person who participated in Feed My Heart!

God To: Kathy O´Grady for her extra support and cover photo

To: The owner of Chilcuague Restaurant and his Chef Sebastian Galvez Conde

To: St. Paul's Church San Miguel Allende www.stpaulsma.com

To: Eric Fash for the editorial design

To: Lighthouse Publishing

Table of Contents:

7	Foreword
8	A Brief History, Tips for Potlucks
9	Main Dishes
53	Daina Testimony
79	Obregon Family Recipes
97	Side Dishes
127	Maawad Family Recipes
141	Desserts
176	Extra Fun Recipes
183	Chef Sebastian Galvez Conde Recipes and Interview
190	Acknowledgments
192	Book Cover Recipes

Foreword:

My experience of how God led me to write this book: The Covid-19 pandemic, which began in 2020 offered an awareness for many of us of what to do in this time. Many lost their health insurance, homes and jobs. It became a worldwide concern. During this time, I was finishing one of my books, *One on One : It's Personal*. My prayers asked for guidance on what to do next. I started to clean and purge what I didn't need from my house. The next thing I knew, I was packing. I left Mexico City and moved to San Miguel Allende. Moving was challenging; I had to remind myself God was with me.

Arriving in San Miguel with few possessions, my faith is what kept me going. God made my journey safe to start a new step in life; I settled in a place where I always wanted to live. At this time, many homes were on the market for sale or for rent. My home in Mexico City was rented sooner then I thought. As a follower of Jesus, I knew God was with me.

So why did I chose to write a cook book? I thoroughly enjoy food, sharing time with people and, of course, cooking. I live in San Miguel, a place where you can find many international dishes to enjoy and also share recipes and fellowship while listening to people's stories.
Foreigners all over the world choose to retire to San Miguel, the "heart of Mexico". The climate in San Miguel relaxes your body while eating outdoors. I hope this book will Bless readers to study what Jesus did when he visited homes, ate and taught his word. This recipe book will support the St. Paul's Church Ministry.

Psalm 37:4 *Delight yourself in the Lord, and he will give the desires of your heart*

A little bit of History

The first recorded female author of a cookbook was the countess of Kent in 1653. Though it was published 2 years after her death, it was quite rare to have a female author, let alone for a cookbook.

One of the first cookbooks I remember owning was written by Betty Crocker. First published in 1950, Betty Crocker was fictitious name developed by Washburn, Crosby Co. It became so successful, it was later a successful brand name for their home baking products. Betty Crocker was even portrayed by several actresses.

Potluck literally means luck of the pot. That is you choose a dish whatever happens to be in the pot. It's a meal or a gathering to which each of the guest contributes a dish. Organized by community groups. A handy tip I learned at the Baptist Church in Mexico City, when you plan a potluck: If you have to transport a hot dish to a potluck, wrap several layers of aluminum foil around the casserole dish, then wrap the dish with a thick towel or several layers of newspapers. Enjoy cooking, by being creative and doing it wholeheartedly serving your love ones by putting a Bless on the table.
A Remembrance of Jesus Luke 22:19 And he took bread, gave thanks and broke it, and gave it to them saying, "This is my body given for you; to do this in remembrance of me."

Main Dishes

Recipe and scripture by Susan Robinson (San Miguel Allende) St. Paul's Church

Psalm 61-verses 2-3
Only in God does my soul rest, from him comes my salvation.
He alone is my rock and my salvation: my fortress: in no wise shall I be moved.

Isaias, chapter 41, verse 10
Fear not, for I am with thee: turn not aside, for I am thy God. I have strengthened thee, and the right hand of my just one hath upheld thee.

TRADITIONAL LASAGNA

From the Collection of Doug Craig

This recipe was copied from Recipe Zaar to use at our first ever Open House in Lewes during the Christmas Season of 2009. I first served it to my Brother (Roger) and Aunt Janetty who visited with us for Roger's and my "Birthday Weekend" in 2009. It got rave reviews from all attendees and with five kinds of cheese it is by far THE BEST lasagna I've ever tasted!

Prep time: 2½ hours | 1¼ hours prep
Expected number of servings: 36 & 12

Ingredients:
1 lb ground beef
¾ lb bulk pork sausage
3 (8 ounce) cans tomato sauce
2 (6 ounce) cans tomato paste
2 garlic cloves, minced.
2 teaspoons sugar
1 teaspoon Italian seasoning
1 teaspoon salt
½ teaspoon pepper
3 eggs (2 oz/egg)
3 tablespoons minced fresh parsley
3 cups small curd cottage cheese
1 (8 ounce) carton ricotta cheese

½ cup grated parmesan cheese
9 lasagna noodles, cooked and drained
6 slices provolone cheese
3 cups shredded mozzarella cheese, divided (12 oz.)

Method:

1. In a skillet, cook beef and sausage over medium heat until no longer pink; drain.

2. Add the next seven ingredients.

3. Simmer, uncovered, for 1 hour, stirring occasionally.

4. In a bowl, combine the eggs and ricotta.

5. Fold in parsley, cottage cheese, and parmesan.

6. Spread 1 cup of meat sauce in an ungreased 13x9x2-inch baking dish.

7. Layer with 3 noodles, provolone cheese, 2 cups of cottage cheese mixture, 1 cup of mozzarella.

8. Then layer with three more noodles, 2 cups of meat sauce, remaining cottage cheese mixture and 1 cup of mozzarella.

9. Top with remaining noodles, meat sauce and mozzarella (dish will be full).

10. Cover and bake at 375°F for 50 minutes.

11. Uncover; bake 20 minutes longer.

12. Let stand 15 minutes before cutting

Recipe By Jonathan Brown St. Paul's Church (San Miguel Allende)

SHRIMP ALA CHRISTINE

Ingredients:

15 Colossal Shrimp (15 Per pound)
Butter
Orange Marmalade (Make sure it has orange rind in it)
Shredded Ginger (Optional)

Method:

Melt butter in a frying pan

Saute the shrimp until they change color

Add three tablespoons of Orange Marmalade (and a teaspoon of shredded ginger to taste)

Stir the mixture until the marmalade is caramelized onto the Shrimp

Serve as an appetizer or as a main dish with Rice

CAMARONES ALA CHRISTINE

Ingredientes:

15 camarones colosales (15 por libra)
Manteca
Mermelada de naranja (asegúrese de que tenga cáscara de naranja)
Jengibre rallado (opcional)

Metodo:

Derretir la mantequilla en una sartén.

Saltear los camarones hasta que cambien de color

Agregue tres cucharadas de mermelada de naranja: (agregue una cucharadita de jengibre fresco rallado al gusto.)

Revuelva la mezcla hasta que la mermelada se carmelice sobre los camarones.

Sirve como aperitivo o como plato principal con Arroz.

Recipe and Scripture By Michael Coon St Paul's Church (San Miguel de Allende)

Romans 12:2 "Don't be conformed to the patterns of this world, but be transformed by the renewing of your minds so that you can figure out what God's will is - what is good and pleasing and mature."

SALMON WITH GINGER SHALLOT VINAIGRETTE

This is one of my favorite recipes that I've prepared for a lot of non salmon lovers with PRAISE. You can also broil it with great success as well. The trick is to under-cook the center.

Ingredients:

1 piece fresh ginger root, about 1 inch long, peeled and minced
2 large shallots, minced
¼ cup rice wine vinegar
2 tablespoons soy sauce
Juice of 2 organic limes
1 cup extra-virgin olive oil, plus 1 tablespoon extra for sautéing
1 tablespoon dark Asian-style toasted sesame oil
Salt
Freshly ground pepper
4 Salmon fillets each about 6 ounces and ½ inch thick
1 bunch fresh cilantro leaves coarsely chipped, plus a few whole leaves reserved for garnish
¼ cup toasted sesame seeds, for garnish

Directions:

In a small mixing bowl, use a wire whisk to stir together the ginger, shallots, vinegar, soy sauce, and lime juice. Whisking vigorously, slowly pour in the olive oil and then the sesame oil. Season to taste with salt and pepper.

Season the fish fillets on three sides with salt and pepper. Heat a large nonstick skillet over high heat. Add the olive oil and the butter and, when the butter has melted, swirl them together to coat the pan and add the fish fillets, cooking them for exactly 3 minutes, flesh side down. Turn heat OFF and cover pan for an additional 3 min and let salmon continue to steam in the covered pan.

As soon as the fish is done, stir the chopped cilantro into the vinaigrette.

Spoon a pool of the vinaigrette in the center of each serving plate. Top each pool of dressing with a fish fillet. Garnish each serving with toasted sesame seeds and a few whole parsley or cilantro leaves.

ENJOY SHARING THE GIFTS GOD GAVE US

Recipe By Jonathan and Quinlan Brown St. Paul's Church (San Miguel de Allende)

BLUE RIBBON CHICKEN (AKA LEMON CHICKEN)

Ingredients:

2 Broiler -Fryers- cut up (or use Boneless Chicken Breasts)
2 Eggs (Beaten)
2 Tbs Milk
1/ ½ Cups Dry Bread Crumbs (Or Crackers)
2 Tsp Grated Lemon Rind (More to Taste – Balance with Lemon Juice)
1 Tsp Salt (You can leave this out if you have used Salted Crackers)
Dash of Pepper
1 Cup (or less) Margarine (Melted)
2 Tbs Lemon juice (More to Taste)

Instructions:

Dip chicken in combined egg and milk, then in mixture of bread crumbs, lemon, rind, and seasonings. Place in baking dish. Combine lemon juice and margarine; pour over chicken Baker at 350 degrees for one hour.

Note: This is a simple but tasty main entree for a dinner party where you do not want to be in the kitchen (I realize in some dinner parties you do but in most you want to be with your guests).

Recipe By Jonathan and Quinlan Brown (San Miguel de Allende)

NO BOIL LASAGNA

Ingredients:

1 box (9 oz) lasagna, uncooked
2 eggs
1 container (15 oz) ricotta cheese
4 cups (16 oz) shredded mozzarella cheese (divided)
½ cup (2 oz) grated parmesan cheese
1 pound Italian sausage or ground beef (cook, crumble, and drain)
2 jar Italian Baking Sauce or Marinara sauce

Instructions:

Preheat oven to 375F

Spray baking pan 9 (13x9x3 inches deep) with non-stick cooking spray.
Remove 16 lasagna sheets from box. DO NOT BOIL.

In medium bowl, beat eggs. Stir in ricotta, 2 cups of mozzarella and the parmesan. (If using a 2 inch deep pan, make three layers to avoid possible boiling over. Use the same amount of filling and 12 uncooked sheets)

When layering the lasagna, slightly overlap sheets. Lasagna will extend to the edges when cooking. Spread filling to edges to seal in and cook the lasagna during baking.

Layer 4 uncooked sheets, ½ ricotta mixture, half of the browned meat,
1 cup mozzarella, and one cup of sauce.
Repeat #2, adding a little more sauce.
Repeat with all remaining ingredients.

Bake, covered with foil, until bubbly, 50-60 minutes. Uncover, and continue cooking until cheese is melted, about 5 more minutes.
Let stand 15 minutes before cutting.
Recipe makes about 12 servings.

Note: This is designed for those working families that want something tasty and simple.

WOODWARD RED CHILI

Ingredients:

1lb. Beef Chuck Roast cut into ½ or ¼ in San Miguel I use New York steak.
½ lb. Ground Chuck
½ lb. Boneless Pork Loin cut into ¼ inch cubes
1 or two onions (white, yellow or purple) finely chopped.
2 to 4 roasted Poblano / Pasilla Chillies. (I roast them on a stove top using a grid)
After chilies are roasted, seal them in a plastic bag and set aside to steam and cool. Once cool, remove seeds and chop to add to sofrito.
1 to 4 roasted jalepeños to taste.
1 or 2 Chipotle Chilies chopped 8 canned in adobe sauce). The rest set aside to offer for variable taste
1 lb. Bag Red Kidney Beans. Or in Mexico, Frijol Ayocote Morado. 8 I have also used small or large Albanias, but the Albanias are tough and need soaking and extra cooking). Soak beans overnight and cook separately from the meat sofrito adding after the beans are done. Otherwise, the meat / sofrito mix may be overcooked as one tries to soften up the beans.
1 box beef broth (optional).
1 Tablespoons Ground Cayenne Pepper 1 bulb of minced garlic to taste
1-2 Tablespoons Cumin Powder
1 or two bottles of Guinness Stout Beer (or equivalent)
1 large can Tomato paste or a box or two of tomato paste or a box or two of tomato sauce, more or less, according to taste, Perhaps chopped tomatoes fresh or canned. This is a meat chilli not a tomato sauce so I see how things are burbling along.
Salt to taste

Prep:

Soak beans overnight and cook separately

Saute onions and garlic in a bit of olive oil or canola oil. Add spices and diced roasted chilies
Put all into sturdy cassoulet on stove with all other ingredients except beans.

Add beer and tomato paste / sauce to taste

Simmer till ready to add cooked beans, and then simmer for beans to absorb flavor

Compliments:

Shredded cheddar cheese, sour cream, avocados, additional chilies

ALLISON MURDOCH'S AMAZING TOMATO PIE

Ingredients:

Crust:

2 c flour
½ c butter (1 stick)
4 t baking powder
¾ c milk (adjust for biscuit dough consistency)
Mix in food processor or by hand.
Divide in half. For bottom and top crusts.

Filling

2 pounds fresh tomatoes, peeled and sliced (or 2 28 oz cans plum tomatoes)
3 Chopped basil, chives, or scallions
1 ½ c sharp cheddar 1/3 c mayonnaise
2 T lemon juice

Instructions:

Roll bottom crust on floured surface and line 9 pie plate. Fill crust with with thinly sliced tomatoes.

Sprinkle with chopped herbs. Cover with 1 cup grated cheddar.

Mix mayonnaise with lemon juice and drizzle over cheese. Cover with remaining ½ c cheddar.

Roll out remaining crust.

Cover pie and pinch the edges to seal. Cut steam vents.

Bake at 400 for about 25 minutes.

If not serving directly from the oven, reheat before serving to melt the cheese.

Recipe by Reverend Canon George F. Woodward III Rector St. Paul's Church (SMA)

BEEF AND MANGO

Ingredients:

3 fresh mangos
12 beef fillet medallions, 4 oz. each
½ Cup Flour
3 Tablespoons butter
1 Cup Champagne
2 Cups Heavy Whipping Cream Salt and pepper

Instructions:

Peel and trim and puree the mangos (some may be sliced and set aside to place on plate) Cover beef medallions in flour. Salt and pepper

Heat the butter in skillet big enough to hold the beef Cook fillets to desired finish over medium heat Remove fillets and set-aside to keep warm

Add the champagne and stir to deglaze skillet skillet Lower heat and add heavy whipping cream

Add pureed mangos Cook until heated through

Spoon mango sauce over beef medallions and serve

Recipe by Reverend Canon George F. Woodward III Rector St. Paul's Church (SMA)

MAC AND CHEESE

Serves 12 Ingredients:
1lb. Or 1 ½ pound of penne pasta (or other shell pasta) 6 cups whole milk
One stick of unsalted butter
½ cup of white flour
½ onion
2 crushed garlics
½ teaspoon cayenne pepper (more to taste)
½ teaspoon dry mustard Dash of nutmeg
Kosher salt to taste
1 or two bricks of sharp cheddar, grated.
1 brick of Tallegio cheese, cut into small cubes.

Instructions:

Dice onion and crush garlic

Add to large pan with one or two sticks of butter and slowly saute Bring mild to a quiet boil in a saucepan and set aside

Make a roux by adding flour to the butter / onion / garlic, whisking constantly

Add milk to the roux, whisking constantly for smooth texture

Add spices Add cheese Cook pasta

Add pasta to cheese sauce and pour into baking dish

Cook in oven between 350 degrees and 400 degrees for 25 minutes or until hot Briefly place under boiler if a browning crust is desired

NICARAGUAN TINGA DE POLLO

Total time: 1 hour 15 minutes, plus cooling time

Servings: 12 Tortillas

Ingredients:

1 pound chicken breasts, bone-in, skin removed

1 bay leaf

1 small white onion
1 cup chopped white onion, divided & thin white onion slices for serving
2 tablespoons vegetable oil
3 tomatoes cored, seeded and chopped
4 teaspoons minced chipotle peppers in adobo, maybe more adobo sauce for serving
½ teaspoon oregano
½ cup chicken broth Salt
12 Corn tortillas cooked or heated on comal 1 cup crema

1 avocado, sliced into slivers
¼ cup crumbles cotija cheese

Instructions:

In a large saucepan, place the chicken breasts and add enough water to cover. Add the bay leaf, unpeeled garlic clove and small chunk of onion and bring to a boil. Cover and remove from heat. Set the pan aside until the chicken has cooked all the way through, about 20 minutes Remove the chicken to a bowl, and set aside until cool enough to handle, the shred the meat with your fingers or a fork.

In a skillet heated over medium-high hear, add the oil. When the oil is hot, add the copped onion and cook until translucent, stirring often, 3 to 5 minutes. Stir in the minced garlic and cook until aromatic, 15 to 30 seconds. Add the tomato, cooking until pieces break down and become a thick, chunky paste, about 5 minutes.

Stir in the shredded chicken, then add the chipotle, oregano and chicken broth,and season with three- fourths teaspoon salt, or to taste. Bring to a boil, then reduce the heat, cover and simmer about 10 minutes to thicken slightly and marry the flavors. Taste, and add more salt if desired. This makes about 2 cups of tinga de pollo.

Tortillas with spoon spoonfuls of tinga, slices of white onion and two silvers of avocado. Top with crumbled cotija cheese.

Recipe and scripture by Lucila Escobedo (Mexico City)

Genesis 43:32 They served him by himself, the brothers by themselves, and the Egyptians who ate with him by themselves, because Egyptians could not eat with the Hebrews, for that is detestable to Egyptians.

SPAGHETTI ESPECIAL

Se cuece el spaghetti normal, se escurre, después en una cacerola se derrite un poco de mantequilla con poca cebolla y se agrega el spaghetti. Se revuelve y se le agrega crema, se vuelve a revolver y por ultimo se le pone cuadritos de jamon delgado y nueces.

Recipe and scripture by Sussy Ramirez St. Paul's Church (San Miguel de Allende)

Mathew 5:27 Oisteis que fue dicho: No cometeras adulterio.

EMPANADAS COLOMBIANAS

Ingredientes para el Relleno:

½ kilo de carne de falda deshebrada
3 papas picadas en cuadritos
1 cucharada de sal
3 cucharadas de aceite
1 cebolla grande picada
½ taza de pimiento rojo picado
Especias al gusto
½ taza de cilantro picado
¼ cucharadita de comino en polvo

Ingredientes para la Masa:

3 tazas de agua templada
1 cucharada de caldo de carne
1 cucharada de sal
2 cucharadas de margarina
3 tazas de harina de maíz
2 cucharadas de harina de trigo
Jugo de limon
Aceite

Preparacion:

Para la masa mezcla las harinas a aparte el agua con el caldo de carne, la sal y el jugo de limon, luego incorpora esta mezcla lentamente a las harinas y añade la margarina hasta lograr una masa muy suave y con una buena consistencia de tal manera que no se pegue en las manos, dejar reposar la masa por media hora a temperatura ambiente.

Aparte hacer un refrito con la cebolla y pimiento rojo finamente picado, agrega las especias, aceite, sal, cilantro y comino, incorpora la carne deshebrada, añade la papa picada en cuadritos pequeños, revuelve todo muy bien y dejar enfriar el guiso por media hora a temperatura ambiente.

Luego toma una cantidad pequeña de masa, extiendela sobre la superficie de un plástico previamente engrasado con aceite y ponle una cuacharada del guiso, dobla y sella mediante un corte semicircular que puedes hacer con un vaso, posteriormente procede a fritarla en aceite con temperatura medio-alta.

Recipe by Lynn Ramsey St. Paul's Church Despensa Project (San Miguel de Allende)

BRISKET

Ingredients:

4 to 5 pound trimmed brisket
Rub course ground pepper all over brisket and press in, use about ¼ cup Marinate
2/3 cup Soy Sauce
½ cup vinegar
1 Tablespoon cátsup
1 Teaspoon Paprika
1 clove garlic

Instructions:

Put in zip lock bags Marinate 24 hours
Wrap brisket in foil and place in a shallow pan
Bake 300 degrees for 3 hours Or 275 degrees for 6 hours I do the 6 hour version

Recipe by Lynn Ramsey St. Paul's Church Despensa Project (San Miguel de Allende)

WHITE BEAN CHILI

This chili, made with chicken and white beans, is creamier and lighter than the traditional chili, very much like a cassoulet, Substitute Great Northern, cannellini, or lima beans for the white beans if desired.

Ingredients:

1 pound dried whit beans
4 cups chicken broth
1 onion, chopped
1 garlic clove, minced
4 cups chopped cooked chicken
4 cups chopped cooked chicken
1 (4 ounce) can chopped green chiles
1 Tablespoon chopped fresh parsley
1 teaspoon (scant) oregano
1/8 teaspoon cayenne pepper
2 cups (12 ounces) shredded Pepper Jack Cheese
1 cup chopped green onions

Instructions:

Sort and rinse beans.

Combine beans with enough water to generously cover in a bowl.
Let stand 8-10 hours, drain.
Combine the beans, broth, onion and garlic in a large heavy saucepan.
Bring to a boil over high heat; reduce the heat.
Simmer for 2 to 3 hours or until the beans are tender, stirring occasionally.
Stir in the chicken, green chili, parsley, oregano and cayenne pepper.
Simmer for 1 hour longer, stirring occasionally.

Ladle into chili bowls. Sprinkle with cheese and green onions.

Recipe and scripture by Marsha Velazquez St. Paul's Church (San Miguel de Allende)

Proverbios 3:5,6 " Confia en el Señor de todo corazón, y no en tu propia inteligencia. Reconocelo en todos tus caminos, y El allanara tus sendas."

CHILE POBLANO " LASANGA "

Rinde 8 a 10 porciones

Ingredients:

6 o 7 chiles poblanos asados, pelados y sin las semillas y venas
2 o 3 tazas de queso cheddar, manchego o chihuahua rallado
4 huevos
4 cucharadas de harina 1 lata de leche evaporada
1 y media tazas de salsa verde

Instruciones:

En un molde de vidrio haz capas de los chiles poblanos y el queso Mezcla los huevos, la harina y la leche y verte la mezcla sobre las capas Hornea 45 mins. A 350 grados F o 180 C. Añadir la salsa verde y hornea 15 mins. Mas.

Recipe By Gwen Rianhard Baptist Church (Ciudad De Mexico)

SHEPHERD'S PIE

Serves 8 to 10

Ingredients:

3 big potatoes peeled cooked and smash
10 spoons of butter and 2 spoons of olive oil
½ cup of milk 700 g minced beef

100 g bacon cut in squares
1 white or yellow medium onion, diced 5 thinly chopped garlic cloves

½ cup grated parmesan cheese
½ cup of a hard cheese like cheddar or gouda
2 sticks of celery thinly sliced
3 medium carrots sliced in small cubes 1 handful of chopped spinach

1 cup of peas
½ cup of red wine for cooking 1 cup of chicken or beef stock 1 spoon of Worcestershire sauce Thyme and Basil

Salt and Pepper to taste

Instructions:

Mashed potatoes:

Melt 8 spoons of butter with the milk and pour them over the mashed potatoes, mix until smooth and creamy texture. Season with salt and pepper and set aside.

Filling:

In a medium big Dutch oven or pot, fry the bacon stirring so it doesn't burn or stick to the pot. When it's cooked and golden remove but leave the melted fat. Add the minced beef to seal and cook, once done remove. Add more olive oil and butter to the pot and cook the onion, garlic, celery and carrots till soft.

Deglaze with the red wine and stir for 5 minutes to simmer . Putt he meat and the bacon back on the pot along with stock, the fine herbs, the peas and the Worcestershire sauce. Stir and let simmer for about 15 minutes till liquids are are almost consumed. Add the spinach, season with salt and pepper. And let cook for a couple of minutes.

Ensemble:

In a ceramic or glass oven-proof dish of 8x8x3 pour the filling around half the height and level. Add the mashed potatoes and level. Cover with the cheese and bake for 20 minutes at 400 degrees.

Let cool for a few minutes, slice and serve. Enjoy!

Recipe and scripture by Jenny Ann Kersten St. Paul's Church San Miguel de Allende

1Corinthians 10:13 " No temptation has seized you except what is common to men. And God is faithful; he will not let let you be tempted beyond what you can bear. But when you are tempted, he will also provide a way out so that you can stand up under it."

JAMBALAYA

Ingredients:

1-1/2 cups diced ham 2 tablespoons oil

½ pound large shrimp, peeled 1-1/2 tablespoons butter

1 medium onions, finely chopped 1 clove garlic, finely minced

2 cup long grain rice
6 cups boiling stock or water 1 can pimento, finely chopped

½ bell pepper

4 small tomatoes, finely chopped or cup canned tomatoes Sale and pepper and cayenne pepper to taste

1 sprigs parsley, finely chopped

Instructions:

Fry the ham and shrimp in the oil; add butter, then the onion and garlic, and saute lightly.

Next, add the rice and saute until golden brown.

Add boiling stock and rest of ingredients; mix well and cover. Let simmer 20 to 25 minutes, or until rice is done.

Recipe and scripture by Jenny Ann Kersten St. Paul's Church (San Miguel de Allende)

1 Corinthians 10:13: No temptation has seized you except what is common to men. And God is faithful; he will not let let you be tempted beyond what you can bear. But when you are tempted, he will also provide a way out so that you can stand up under it.

STUFFED ARTICHOKES

Serves 4
Ingredients:
1 large artichoke.

Stuffing:

3 Tbsp. Butter
3 green onions (including tops), chopped fine
1 c. mushrooms chopped fine
1c. shredded, mild Cheddar cheese
½ c. bread crumbs
½ tsp. salt
1/8 tsp. chervil (or marjoram) Good dash of black pepper
2 egg. Well beaten
½ c. sour cream Grated cheese Drawn butter

Instructions:

With scissors clip the tops from 4 large artichokes. Cut off the stems and, with a melon ball maker, scoop out the "chokes." Only cut down to the bottom of the artichokes; do not cut into it. Stand artichokes upright in a pan and cook in plenty of boiling, salted water with a slice of lemon and a clove or two of garlic. Boil from 25 to 40 minutes, according to size. Drain upside down on paper towels.

When cool enough to handle spread apart the leaves slightly so the stuffing can be easily put in the center hole.

Stuffing: Braise until clear the butter and onions. Add the mushrooms and cook for 2 minutes more. Add the shredded cheese, bread crumbs, salt, chervil, and pepper; mix well. Mix together the eggs and sour cream and add to the cheese mixture.

Stuff the artichokes with this mixture. Remove skin form the stems if it is tough. Chop stems and put on top of stuffing. Add some grated cheese. Bake at 400 degrees for 30 minutes. Serve with small dish of drawn butter for dipping artichoke leaves.

Recipe and scripture by Jenny Ann Kersten St. Paul's Church (San Miguel de Allende)

1 Corinthians 10:13: No temptation has seized you except what is common to men. And God is faithful; he will not let let you be tempted beyond what you can bear. But when you are tempted, he will also provide a way out so that you can stand up under it.

LASAGANA A LA MEXICANA
Heat oven to 375F Serves 8

Ingredients:

8 oz no boil lasagna noodles (if using regular lasagna noodles, prepare noodles as package directs, drain)
1 lb. Lean ground beef
½ cup chopped onion
½ cup chopped green bell pepper 2- ½ cups salsa (approx. 24 oz.)
7 oz. can whole kernel corn, drained 1 tsp. Chili powder
1 cup (6 oz.) ricotta cheese or cream style cottage cheese 1 cup (4 oz.) shredded cheddar cheese
1-1/4 oz. Can sliced ripe olives, drained 1 cup (4 oz.) shredded cheddar cheese Sour cream

Instructions:
In a 10 – inch skillet brown ground beef, onion and green pepper drain off fat. Return beef mixture to skillet.
Add salsa, corn and chili powder.
Combine ricotta and one cup cheddar cheese.
In a 13 x9 -inch baking dish, layer one third of the meat sauce, half of the Lasagna and half of the combined cheeses. Repeat layers ending with sauce.

Sprinkle olives and remaining cup of shredded cheese. Cover with foil and bake 30 minutes
Let stand 10 minutes before serving Garnish with sour cream
Options: Can also be made with tortillas in place of lasagna noodles

Recipe by Jenny Kersten St. Paul's Church (San Miguel de Allende)

SPAGHETTI MEAT SAUCE, BOLOGNESE STYLE

Ingredients:

2 Tablespoons chopped yellow onion
4 Tablespoons olive oil
3 Tablespoons butter
1 Carrot, chopped
1 celery stalk, chopped
¾ Pound ground lean beef 1 tablespoon salt
1 Cup dry white wine
½ Cup milk
1/8 teaspoon nutmeg
1 28 oz. can Italian tomatoes, crushed, with their juice
1 8 oz. can tomato sauce
1 teaspoon sugar
1 Tablespoon Italian herb seasoning

Instructions:

Put the onion, oil and butter in a heavy, enameled cast iron pot and saute briefly over medium heat until just translucent.

Add celery and carrot and cook gently for 2 minutes.

Add the ground beef, crumbling it in the pot with a fork.

Add the salt stir and cook only until the meat has lost its raw, red color

Add the wine. turn the heat up to medium high, and cook, stirring occasionally, until all the wine has evaporated.

Turn the heat down to medium, add the milk and the nutmeg and cook until the milk has evaporated. Stir frequently.

When the milk has evaporated add the tomatoes, sauce, sugar sugar and seasoning stir thoroughly.

When the tomatoes have started to bubble, turn the heat down until the sauce cooks at the laziest simmer, with just an occasional bubble.

Cook uncovered, for a minimum of 3-1/2 to 4 hours, stirring occasionally

Taste and correct for salt

Recipe by Jenny Kersten St. Paul's Church (San Miguel de Allende)

THAI STIR FRY OVER BASMATI RICE W/ MIXED GREEN SALAD

We recommend the finest ingredients you can find organic if possible. To bring out the fullest flavors of this recipe. Earth Song market has all of these ingredients and the finest selection of organic produce available in the county. This is a first-class meal and will please not only the palate but the eye as well.

Ingredients:

Thai Peanut Ginger Sauce
5 oz. fresh ginger (approx ½ lb)
12 cloves garlic (fresh)
¼ cup canola oil
¼ cup sesame oil
1 cup raw light bodied honey (clover)
1 cup rice vinegar
1 ½ cup natural peanut butter (no additives or sugars 1 ½ cup tamari
¾ TSP cayenne
Peel and slice ginger in ¼ rounds, peel garlic, blend all ingredients together in food processor or blender.

Veggie Sautee

1 head purple cabbage sliced thin
2 large heads broccoli
2 lbs cut to tops. Peel and slice stems
2 large red bell peppers in long thin slices
1 lb. Button mushrooms in ¼ slices
Sautee in hot olive oil, slat and pepper to taste rice (Basmati) or noodles

Salad

1 mescal salad mix

2 carrots shredded

Salad dressing of choice (recommend balsamic vinaigrette)

Beverage of choice (recommend Oregon chai mix – from earth song market and either milk or soy milk to mix with it for a perfect after dinner beverage)

This recipe is for approx. 4 adults. The sauce will make enough to serve 4 guests 3 or 4 times depending on the quantity used, but since it is time consuming and we are sure you will like it. We recommend saving the rest for another dinner soon.

HERBED NOODLES

Ingredients & instructions:

12 oz. package wide egg noodles
Cook according to package

directions

¼ cup butter (½ stick)
¼ cup flour, all purpose
1 cup heavy cream, heated
1 cup milk, heated
Melt butter in heavy saucepan Add flour, whisk to incorporate
Add cream and milk in a slow, Whisk till smooth.
Cook over low to medium hear until sauce thickens

1 tsp. ea Thyme, Basil , Summer Savory, Chives, Parsley 1-1/2 cup Grated sharp cheddar cheese
Stir herbs and 1 cup cheese into milk mixture. Salt and Pepper, to taste
Mix noodles with cheese sauce. Top with remaining ½ cup cheese.
Place under broiler or put into microwave oven to melt cheese, if needed.

Recipe by: Stephenie Sedacey (San Miguel Allende)

John 3:16   ""For God so loved the world that he gave his one and only Son, that whoever believes in him shall not perish but have eternal life.""

ESCABECHE – BELIZEAN ONION SOUP

Ingredients:

1 whole chicken
6-8 whole allspice seeds
6 oregano leaves or
2 tsp crushed oregano
6 whole cloves
1 teaspoon – cumin seeds
2 teaspoons – whole peppercorn
1 stick – cinnamon
1 tablespoon – Consume de Pollo Maggi or Knorr (preferred brands)
Salt and pepper to taste
4 cloves garlic
2-4 lbs. white onions thinly sliced
1 cup – Distilled white vinegar, a little more or less depending on your taste
1 small can of pickled jalapeños or
2-4 whole fresh jalapeños
Seasoning for chicken – seasoned salt (we like Lawry Seasoned Salt), Lee and Perrins, olive oil or butter

Instructions:

Part 1: Prep the Chicken
Wash your chicken in water and lime juice, and trim off any fat and chicken slime. Split the chicken in half the chicken and place in a 6-quart heavy soup pot.
Add water to the pot covering the chicken, OR until it's half full, OR you can calculate 1 1/2 cups liquid per person.
Bring the water and chicken to a simmer, adding the spices: allspice, oregano, cloves, cumin, pepper, cinnamon stick, Consume de Pollo Maggi, and garlic.
Simmer for 30-45 minutes.
We have found that the chicken will cook in 30 minutes, but has a better texture if simmered for 45 minutes.
Part 2: Prep the Onion
While the chicken is cooking blanch the onions.

Put a kettle of water on to boil. Peel and slice onions, separate the onion slice layers in a large bowl. When slicing the onions keep in mind your desired level of al dente. We prefer thin slices over thick. We like them about 1 to 2 millimeters wide.
Pour boiling water over onions, and allow onions to sit in water until the chicken is cooked, then drain (Part 2 B).

ESCABECHE – BELIZEAN ONION SOUP (Continued)

Instructions:

Part 3: Broil the Boiled Chicken
Preheat broiler to medium or high. 550 degrees works well.
Using tongs, pull the chicken out of the simmering broth and place on a cookie sheet to be broiled or grilled. Allow any excess liquid to remain in the pot.
If you want to breakdown the chicken in portions this is a good time to do it. Place the chicken skin-side up on the baking sheet.
Next, baste the chicken with an emulsion of Worcestershire sauce like Lee and Perrins sauce, and olive oil or butter. We prefer olive oil.
Sprinkle the chicken with seasoned salt. We like Lawry's seasoned salt. Place under broiler for 10-15 minutes or until the skin is golden brown.

Part 2 B: Finishing the Onions in the Soup
Drain the blanched onions and place them in chicken broth (this step happens after the chicken is removed). Add vinegar and jalapeños.
Allow onions to cook for 15-30 minutes, 15 minutes if you like your onions crunchier. If desired, add more vinegar to taste.
Serve soup with a piece of roasted chicken and a few warm corn tortillas.

As the onions are cooking we typically are broiling the chicken. Keep in mind the cook times. You may want to delay broiling while your onions are cooking for a few minutes. The goal is to make crispy delicious chicken skins not burned chicken. This is a step that sets this recipe apart and is a huge enhancement in flavor and texture. Count on the colonial British influence and Mayan culture mashing up to make for intense flavors. We serve this soup piping hot with a piece of chicken and fresh corn tortillas. We like to dress with a big sprinkle of freshly ground black pepper. In Belize, this will always be served with an ice-cold Coke.

Recipe by: Robert Diaz del Campo (San Miguel Allende)

RABBIT, HUNTER STYLE

This recipe is in English and Spanish

Cut a rabbit weighing 1 kilo into big pieces and let him marinate for 12 hours in ½ litre of dry red wine with salt, peeper thyme, bay, sage and marjoram. In a wide iron frying pan with 80 gm of butter and 1 glass full of oil, fry 4 small sliced onions, to which you will add one carrot, 2 celery sticks and one clove of garlic. Separately heat the rabbit and sprinkle it over with a hint of white flour. Add the meat to the vegetables, then thin with the marinate and cook on a low flame. When half done, sieve the sauce and add the rabbit víscera heart, kidneys and liver.

Let the sauce thicken, 40 minutes cooking time will be enough to cook the rabbit.

CONEJO A LA CAZADORA

Desmembrar un conejo de 1kg en sus piezas mas grandes: muslos, pecho, cabeza, etc. Frotar cada una de las piezas con una mezcla fina de pimienta, tomillo, mejorana y salvia
y luego ponerlo a macerar, de un dia para el otro. Casi 12 horas, en medio litro de vino rojo seco con una hojas de laurel y un poco de sal. Al momento, de sacarlo para cocinarlos se debería tener una olla de bordes altos con un vaso de aceite de oliva con 80 gm de mantequilla en el que vamos a saltear cebolla en rebanadas muy finas, agregando después dos ramos de apio en rebanadas delgadas, una zanahoria rebanadas y und diente de ajo bien picado. Por separado en otra cacerola o sarten, se deberán escaldar o freir ligeramente las piezas del conejo. Luego que esten listas se deberán cubrir de harina y depositarlas en el recaudo de las verduras al que se le debería agregar el vino de la marinada. Comenzar a cocinar a,
fuego lento, a mitad de cocimiento se deberán agregar las vísceras, corazón, hígado, y riñones, y continuar, cocinando por 40 min. Apagar la preparación y esperar un rato antes de servir.

Recipe and scripture By: Sandra Orellana Writer (San Miguel Allende)

Ecclesiastes 9:7 " Go, eat your food with gladness and drink your wine with a joyful heart."

MOLE VERDE CON POLLO
Ingredients:

Onion Lettuce
Green tomatoes Garlic
Green pepita (in powder) Chile jalepeño
Cilantro
Saltine Crackers (crushed) The key that made my grandmother's recipe different was using saltine crackers. Place all ingredients except green pepita and saltine crackers into a blender and blend with chicken broth. Fry the green pepita in a pan and crushed saltine crackers (I use olive oil) Then pour the blended ingredients into the pan with the green pepita. (all together in the pan) and start to stir about 30 min. flavor will be better (You can stir less). While you're stirring, you can add more olive oil and salt. Serve with chicken. Note: Make it a day before serving for a better flavor.

Recipe and scripture by: Karen Wilson (Michigan)

Matthew 4:4 "But he answered and said, It is written, Man shall not live by bread alone, but by every word that proceedeth out of the mouth of God."

SPICY CROCKPOT WHITE BEAN CHILE

48 oz jar great Northern beans 16 oz medium salsa
16 oz. Hot salsa or another medium salsa 4 oz. diced green chiles
4 oz. 4 oz. diced jalapeños
8 oz. 8 oz. Jack cheese cut into chunks
1 store- bought rotisserie chicken skinned and shredded 1 cup chicken broth or bone broth
Sour cream garnish Tortilla chips garnish Jalapeños garnish
Chopped red onion garnish

Instructions:

Combine all ingredients except garnishes in a slow cooker.
Cook on low for 4 to 5 hours.
Serve up with desired garnishes and cornbread or a salad!
Note: If it's a bit thick for leftovers, just add the optional chicken broth to thin it out.

Recipe by: Connie Hebert B.A. M.S.W. (San Miguel Allende)

CAJUN GUMBO RECIPE (IN ENGLISH AND SPANISH)

Ingredients:

1 cup of white flour and one cup of oil (I use olive oil) but other oils work as well)
1 cup of each chopped vegetable:
Onion, bell pepper, and celery. Main ingredient: shrimp, oyster,
Chicken, pork sausage. Single or combination
2 cups of white rice (cheat and use brown rice, but the original recipe is white rice.)
File gumbo (sassafras) to taste

Directions:

Pour white flour and oil into heated pot (iron if you can find it).

Stir consistently under a high fire until the combination (known as roux is very dark, (just before burning) If you burn the roux, start over.

Add your main ingredient to the roux and sautee until cooked. Add vegetables when the main ingredient is cooked.

Add hot water (to about 1 inch over the main ingredient and vegetables) Lower the heat and cook at a slow simmer until done. Cook rice while gumbo is simmering.

Serve:

Serve rice into bowl until half-filled (that´s you want to have more rice than in regular rice dishes. Then pour hot gumbo over rice. Optional: Serve with sweet potatoes or potato salad.

RECETA DE GUMBO CAJUN (En Español)

Ingredientes:

1 taza de harina blanca y una taza de aceite (uso aceite de oliva) pero otros aceites también funcionan) 1 taza de cada vegetal picado: cebolla, pimiento y apio.

Ingrediente principal: camarones ,ostras, pollo, salchicha de cerdo. Sencillo o combinado 2 Tazas de arroz blanco (hago trampa y uso arroz integral, pero la receta orginal es arroz blanco.

Archivo gumbo (sassafras) al gusto

Indicaciones:

Vierta la harina blanca y el aceite en la olla calentada (hierro si puede encontrarlo) Revuelva constantemente bajo un fuego alto hasta que la combinación (conocida como roux) sea muy oscura ,(justo antes de quemar) Si quemas el roux, empieza de nuevo. Agregue su ingrediente principal al roux y sofríe hasta que este cocido. Agregue las verduras cuando se cocine el ingrediente principal. Añadir agua caliente (a aproximadamente 1 pulgada sobre el ingrediente principal y verduras) Baje el fuego y cocine a fuego lento hasta que este hecho. Cocine el arroz mientras el gumbo esta cocinando al fuego lento.

Servir: Sirva el arroz en un tazon hasta que este medio lleno (asi es, desea tener mas arroz que arroces regulares.

Luego vierta gumbo caliente sobre el arroz. Opcional: Sirva con batatas o ensalada de papas.

Receta y escritura de: Rosario Gomez (Ciudad de Mexico)

Psalm 119:37 Aparta mis ojos de cosas inútiles, y dame vida mediante tu palabra.

TACOS DE PESCADOS

Para 4 personas
Ingredientes:

4- Filetes Pescado Bazza Harina
Pan molido para pescado
1 huevos

Procedimiento:

Cortar en tiras el filete se agrega pimienta y sal al gusto salsa maggi y inglesa. Se bate el huevo y se agrega sal y pimienta al gusto. Se en harina las tiras y después se pasan por el huevo y al final en el pan se fríen en el sarten con bastante aceite, se colocan en toallas absorventes .
Ensalada como guarnición col, pepino , zanahoria rayada agregar oregano y sal

Salsas 2 tipos:

1 mayonesa con chipotle
2 jarabe tamarindo con chipotle ambos mezclarlos.

Recipe and scripture by: Jennifer Morrison Missions for Life - Love One Another (Delaware, United States)

Isaiah 40:31 but those who hope in the Lord will renew their strength. They will soar on wings like eagles; they will run and not grow weary, they will walk and not be faint.

CHICKEN PICCATA WITH ARTICHOKES

Ingredients:

2 chicken breasts, butterflied and pounded thin
Sea salt and fresh ground pepper 2 Tbs of flour
6 Tbs of butter
5 Tbs extra virgin olive oil 1/3 cup fresh lemon juice 1/2 cup chicken stock
1/2 cup chicken stock
1/4 cup of brined capers rinsed
1 (12 ounce) jar of marinated artichoke hearts , drained 1/3 cup of fresh chopped parsley

Directions:

Season chicken with salt and pepper, then dredge in flour.

In a large skillet over medium heat, Melt 4 tablespoons of butter with 5 tablespoons of Olive oil. Cook chicken until lightly browned, about 3 min. on each side. Remove and transfer to a plate.

Add lemon juice, chicken stock, capers and artichokes to the pan. Bring to a boil. Return the chicken to the pan and simmer for another 5 min. Remove chicken, then add 2 tablespoons of butter and whisk.

Pour over chicken, garnish with parsley. Serve with pasta, rice or mashed potatoes.

Receta de : Sylivia Muller (Cuidad de Mexico)

PESCADO A LOS 3 CHILES

Ingredientes Para

Marinar:

1 kg de lomo de robalo cortado en filetes lavado y sin sangre
1 C de sal
2 pz. De limon
Tajin
1 C de harina para el pyrex
1/2 taza de aceite de olivo para hornear el pescado

Para Licuar:

½ taza de aceite de olivo
2 dientes de ajos fileteados 1/4 de cebolla
4 pz. De chile ancho sin semillas y cortados en tiras delgadas con tijeras
4 pz. De chile cguajillos sin simillas y cortados en tiras delgadads con tijeras
5 pz. De chile pasilla sin smillas y cortados en tiras delgadas con tijeras
1 C de Sal
1 taza de jugo de naranja
2 pza de limones exprimidos sin semillas
1 c. de consome

Decoracion:
1/2 Taza de hojas de perejil finamente picado

Modo de elaboración:

Lavar el pescado y dejarlo limpio, ponerle sal, limones, Tajoin y marinarlo agregándole la cascara del limon por 15 min.

Rociar un poco de harina en el pyrex y colocar los filetes ya marinados, agregar el aceite para que se cosan, en el horno a 200 grados centígrados

Calentar el aceite de olivo freir el ajo y sacarlo cuando se dore, ahí mismo freir los chiles sin dejar de mover por 5 segundos cuidar que no se quemen, ahí mismo freir la cebolla , dejar que se dore y sacarlo Licuar con el mismo aceite donde se frio todo, la mitad de los chiles con la naranja , el limon la cebolla el ajo la sal y el consome y calentar la salsa por 15 min.

Cambiarle el aceite al pescado y agregar el aceite con los chiles licuados y el resto de los chiles encima caliente, decorar con perejil finamente picado

Hornear 5 min. mas y servir caliente.

Receta de: Veronica Yañez Datos: Instagram productos y teléfono: 56962399262 (Santiago de Chile)

COMIDAS CHILENAS

Ingredientes

2 tazas de porotos blancos Aceite o Manteca
250 grs de zapallo calabaza Tallarines No 5
4 longanizas
1 Cebolla mediana
2 dientes de ajo
1 trozo de pimenton rojo Aji de color a gusto Comino a gusto Oregano a gusto

Preparacion

Dejamos remojando los porotos desde la noche anterior. Al dia siguiente lavamos los porotos y los estilamos, mientras tanto pelamos el zapallo y lo cortamos en trozos uniformes o cuadrados pequeños.

Cocina los porotos junto con el zapallo en una olla tradicional grande por lo menos 1 hora hasta que queden blandos o si eliges la olla a presión, también en abundante agua fría, por unos 40 minutos, ambas cocciones con un poco sal y un diente de ajo.

Por otro lado freir la cebolla con ajo, comino, oregano, piementon, sal y aji de color, revolver con cuchara de madera, agregar las longanizas trozadas en laminas regulares o enteras, dejar que sulten todo su jugo y se impregnen bien todos los sabores.

Cuando los porotos están listo se le incorpora el sofrito y un puñado de tallarines Numero 5 (gustas puedes cortarlos por la mitad) dejar cocinar unos 10 min. Mas, revolviendo para que no se pegue.

Recuerda siempre ajustar sazon y lograr una textura cremosa. Dejar reposar y servir el plato, preferentemente en una fuente de greda.

Recipe by: Vanessa D' Rand (San Miguel Allende)

SPICY SALMON VERACRUZ

4 salmon steaks of equal size
1 pound Cherry or grape tomatoes 4 cloves garlic, sliced thin
4 shallots, sliced thin
1/ 2 cup pimiento-stuffed olives , sliced thin 1/4 cup extra-virgin olive oil
1/3 cup sherry vinegar
3/4 cup fresh basil, chopped 1 jalapeno and minced
Salt and pepper

Adjust oven rack to lowest position, preheat oven to 500 degree F (260)

Mix all ingredients but the salmon in a large bowl, including a generous sprinkling of salt and pepper. Cut for pieces of heavy-duty aluminum foil into 12 x 18 (30 x45 cm) sizes and place one salmon steak on each piece of foil. Place equal amounts of the mixture on the salmon. Bringing the long sides of the foil together, fold over 1/2 inch and crimp. Do the same thing two additional times. Fold the ends in twice to seal completely.

Place the foil packets on a rimmed baking sheet and bake for 15 min. Let stand unopened for 3 min. Then serve immediately. Add a garnish with basil, if desired.

Receta by: Marcela Jimenez Cortes (Cuidad de Mexico)

POLLO A LA CERVEZA CON GUAJILLO

Ingredientes

1 Pollo en Piezas
1 Cebolla Picadita
2 dientes ajo picaditos
2 chiles guajillos asados y remojados en agua caliente
1 cerveza coronita
¼ kilo papitas cambray cocidas y peladas

Dorar el pollo un poco en un poco de aceite y sacarlo

Acitronar la cebolla y ajo, agregar los chiles y cerveza y dejar a que los chiles esten suaves. Moler en la licuadora y condimentar consal y pimienta, freir la salsa, agregar el pollo y cebollitas y las papitas cocidas y peladas …Servir con los rabos de las cebollitas picaditos para adornar.

Recipe and scripture by: Johanna Kooleman Beynen (Washington D.C.)

Matthew 5:6 Blessed are those who hunger and thirst for righteousness, for they will be filled.

ORIENTAL CHICKEN w/ BROCCOLI

4 servings

2 boneless, skinless chicken breasts, cut in cubes, marinate in 6 tbs soya sauce,
6 tbs mirin wine
(or sherry or shaoxing wine)20 min.

Meantime, cut up 1 large head of broccoli, 1 medium yellow onion, make sauce of 1 tbs cornstarch,

1bs sesame oil, ½ tbs Worcestershire sauce. Heat a large frying pan, fry onion over medium high until translucent, add chicken, and 1 tbs chopped garlic. When chicken is cooked through, add broccoli, marinade, and sesame oil sauce, cook over medium-low heat until broccoli is just tender, add chili flakes to taste, serve over rice.

Recipe and scripture By: Janice Driscol (San Miguel Allende)

CHICKEN CROQUETTES

You first need to make one cup of thick White sauce.

You make the thick white sauce with 1/4 cup of flour, 1/4 of butter melted, a quarter teaspoon of salt, and eighth of a teaspoon of pepper.

You put these in a sauce pan and heating it while stirring, until it's a little bubbly.

Then you add one cup of milk and you keep stirring until it becomes thickened then you put that aside. In

a large bowl, mix together 2 cups chicken trap chicken K 1 tablespoon of minced onion one teaspoon

of snipped parsley add some salt and pepper mix these together and then add the thick white sauce and stir together.

You will then take this mixture and put it in a shallow glass dish that you would use to bake in the oven cover this and put it in the refrigerator for at least 3 hours after 3 hours you will take it out of the refrigerator and divide the mixture into 12 equal parts.

Then you will take one egg and two tablespoons of water and beat those together and three quarter cup of dry bread crumbs in another dish. Your will take one of these equal parts roll in your hand and then dip it in the egg and water mixture and then roll hit in they dry bread crumbs. Put these 12 they look like little round balls on a plate cover them and put them in the refrigerator for another 2 hour. Then you will take the and you want to at deep fry them and 365 degrees in a deep fat fryer or kettle you only need to deep fry them for about 2 min. till they are light brown and take them out, drain them and keep your croquettes warm until you're going to serve them.

Receta y escritura de : Chris Fernandez Tenista (Cuidad de Mexico)

Salmo 143:8 Hazme oir por la mañana tu misericordia, Porque en ti he confiado; Hazme saber el camino por donde ande, Porque a ti he elevado mi alma.

FRIJOL CON PUERCO

Espulgue el frigol. Lavelo varias veces y cocínelo en suficiente agua y poca sal. El puerco cortelo en persas regulares, y remójelo unos minutos con sal.
Cuando el frijol haya hervido lo suficiente, anadale el puerco, media cebolla asada y hojas de cebolla. Pruebe el punto de sal, agréguele el apazote y cuando la carne este bien cocida, escurrala y póngala en otra sarten; tabela bien.

Deje que frijol termine de cocinarse , hasta que espese lo necesario.
Prepare el salpicon, picando menudidto la cebolla, cilantro y rabanos bien lavados; ruedas de limon y de chile habanera acomoda el sal picon en un plato plano, pon en centro todo lo picadilto y en las orillas del plato las ruedas de limon y de chile habanero.

Los tomates aselos al carbon, estando fríos se pelan, y luego tamuletos con un chile habanero asado, si la agrada el picante, pónganle y sal .

Receta y escritura de: Lic. Enfermeria y Tanatologa Jaqueline Salgado 415-1250399 (San Miguel Allende)

Filipenses 4:13 Todo lo puedo en Cristo que me fortalece.

REJAS CON CREMA

6 Chiles poblanos
1 cuarto de crema
1 latita de elotes Sal al gusto
Un ¼ de cubo de Knorr Suiza

Se asan los chiles y se pelan, se lavan y se quitan semillas y venas. En un sarten se calenta y se pone la crema, se cortan los chiles en rajas, se pone el elote con la crema y se agragan las rajas.

Se pone sal y Knorr suiza con un poco de oregan se mezcla todo a esperar que hierva y listo.

Recetas de: Coco (San Miguel Allende)

MOLE DE OLLA

Ingredientes:

5 chiles anchos
2 papas
5 chiles pasilla ejotes al gusto
5 Chiles guajillo elote partido en rodajas
Pizca de comino un ramo grande de epazote
Pizca de pimienta
3 calabacitas en rodaja o cortadas al gusto
Pizca de oregano
1 cebolla medinana
3 dientes de ajo grandes
1 kg de chambaret con o sin hueso (según gusto)

Se asan los chiles y se desvenan si no lo quieren picoso, si lo quieren picoso se la dejan las venas, se pone agua a hervir y ahí se remojan los chiles por 10 min. se pone después de remojados en la licuador con los demás ingredientes, c de preferencia se asa el ajo y cebolla.
La carne de pone a coser en olla express por una hora y se le cuela todo lo que se molio en la licuadora y se te pone la verdura, lavada y cortada al gusto.

Despues de cocia la carne se le agregan las verduras y un ramo grande de epazote, y se deja cocer en la olla por 15 o 20 min. mas.
Se sirve muy caliente un trozo de carne con verdura de toda la que se uso y el epazote de saca y se le pone limon si se desea.

Receta de: Marcela Jimenez Cortez (Cuidad de Mexico)

SPAGAHETTI CON CHILE POBLANO

500 gr. Spaghetti
7 chiles poblanos asados y desvenados 1 dente ajo y media cebolla
1 taza leche
1 queso crema grande
½ litro de crema
200 grs. Queso amarillo rallado una barrita mantequilla

Poner a cocer el spaghetti en una olla con bastante agua hirviendo y sal

Mientras tanto licuar los chiles con el ajo, cebolla y leche, añadir el queso crema y condimentar con consome en polvo y volver a licuar

En una cacerola poner mantequilla y freir lo licuado, agregar la crema y rectificar sal y pimienta Escurrir el spaghetti y reservar una taza del liquido, poner en el refractario untado de mantequilla y agregar la salsa , revolver, si es necesario agregar el agua que reservamos y poner el queso rallago encima, gratinar en el horno.

Receta de: Anel Nancy Lopez Hernandez Tenista (Cuidad de Mexico)

PUERCO AL CHILAJO O EN CHILE AMARILLO

Esta receta es típica de Oaxaca

Ingredientes:

1 kg de carne de puerco
5 tomates
100gramos de chile costeño amarillo, si no hay chile amarillo puede ser guajillo
4 dientes de ajo grandes
Una trozo de cebolla
Consoe en polvo o cubos al gusto Comino, una pizca
4 Pimientas gordas

Preparacion:

Se lava la carne perfectamente bien, ya que este bien lavada, la ponemos a cocer como usualme lo hacemos, cuando este, reservamos la carne y el caldo por separado. Ponemos a cocer el tomate y el chile costeño en un poco del caldo del puerco (si es con guajillo, tostar los chiles un poco después de limpiarlos)
En una cacerola ponemos a freir la carne para que dore, mientras licuamos el tomate, los chiles, el ajo, cebolla , el comino y las pimientas. Vaciamos en la cacerola y sazonamos. Y eso es todo, podemos agregar verdolagas, espinacas, papas, champiñones, calabazas, u otra verdura y legumbre de nuestra preferencia.

Notes:

Daina Jazmin Ventura's Testimony

Recipe, scripture and testimony by : Daina Jasmine Ventura (San Miguel Allende) 998 121 2771 (if you would like to order a warm meal and delivered.) Daina Facebook: Rico!@REGIONALITALITALIANACOOKING

1 Corinthians 16:14 Let all that you do be done in love.
Cooking for Drew

 I'm Italian, but God guided me to move and live in San Miguel de Allende – Mexico 8 years ago , together with my then 84 years old mom with dementia.
In San Miguel I found a family, a church, a new purpose and many many Friends. Drew Arnold was one of them, but more than that, he has been a role model, a hero:
He suffered from Multiple Sclerosis and , since 2011 he was living in Rancho Los Labradores, where he courageously moved from the USA, together with his beloved wife Mary.

He was a remarkable man, in spite of his atrocious disease, which was forcing him on a wheelchair and able to move just a few fingers of his right hand and barely speak, he committed and succeeded to live his life fully till his last breath, following Jesus all the way and not the easy one. He has been an example to many and worked hared every day to accomplish with many tasks: helping a Christian Church and a Scholl. Always in awe for the beauty of creation, always smiling to everyone, encouraging everyone, loving everyone.
When Mary had to go away for short times, she asked some of their Friends to help cooking and feeding Drew in his home. I eagerly accepted, not just to serve him, but especially to enjoy his precious company. He has always been a sport with a good sense of humor and even when you thought you were on the verge of tears, he was the one to make you laugh.

Drew loved food, especially Italian food, since it reminded him the time he spent there with Mary in their youth, cycling on the Alps.

So, whenever I went to cook for him I made him Lasagna and tiramisu and his smile grew bigger than ever. Drew left this world in November of 2018, he went home to our Heavenly Father, where he was often saying he was ready to go…

He is great missed, but always be remembered.

LASAGNA WITH MEAT SAUCE: RAGU (or BOLOGNESE)

Let's start with the Italian "Trinity "…no worries it´s not some sort of heresy…
It's the Italian base for any sauce or cooked meal: Onion, carrot, celery (you might add or substitute onion with garlic) finely chopped and saute the in another "must have" for Italians : Extra virgin Olive Oil (EVO from now on).

When the Trinity is softened and goldened (not brown!)
You can add whatever else you want in the sauce.
In this case we'll add ground beef until browned.
Then you might add half glass of White or red wine.

When it's dry, add the tomatoes puree (I use CIRO, which can be found at Soriana) add salt and pepper and herbs to taste and cook on low fire, covered for at least 90 minutes (simmering now and then not letting it stick to the pan).

If the sauce gets too dry or thins too much add some more wine or some broth, or the salted boiling wáter in which you'll boil the noddles, till its ready.
You can add some oregano or basil to taste.
Meanwhile prepare the bechamel sauce: note that I use EVO instead of butter, or half and half.
Ingredients: 300 ml of milk, 2 or 3 tablespoons extra virgin olive oil, and / or chunk of butter , a cup of flour, salt and nutmeg to taste.

Preparation: In a small saucepan pour the EVO/butter and flour; puto n the heat to very low and amalgamate the ingredients well using a whip. Slowly add the mild, stirring constantly cook low fire for a couple of minutes without bringing to a boil. Season with salt, pepper and nutmeg.

MAKING LASAGNA:

Ingredients (serve 8 -10 people)
I use ready to bake whole wheat lasagna De Cecco or De Lallo (at Mega) but you can use other types of lasagna or make it yourself.
First of all, put some water with a spoon of salt (better if kosher) to boil in a low pan on medium-high fire, to precook the lasagna even if it says it's ready to bake, this few minute cooking makes them softer. Careful not to make them stick.

Receta de: Eduardo Angeles Garcia dueño y entrenador de Tenis (Cuidad de Mexico) PIZZARETAS (nombre del negocio) 555- 615-6200 (si quieres hacer un pedido o clases de Tenis)

PIZZARETA ESPECIAL

Jamon serrano champinon, pimiento verde, cebolla, chorizo y lomo canadiense

Recipe by: Linda Warren (San Miguel Allende)

ENCHILADA WITH PUMPKIN SEED SALSA

Total 30 min, / serves 4

Ingredients

8 soft corn tortillas
1 large white onion
2 peppers (1 each red and yellow), quartered 2 1/2 Tbsp vegetable oil
Kosher salt and pepper
1/2 cup corn kernels, thawed it frozen
3 oz Monterey Jack cheese, coarsely grated (about 3/4 cup) 1 cups packed cilantro, roughly chopped
1 jalapeño, finely chopped (seeded, if desired)
2 tsp light brown sugar 1/4 tsp ground turmeric
1/2 cup raw pumpkin seeds
4 Tbs fresh lime juice (from 3 to 4 limes) 1 beefsteak tomato, roughly chopped

Directions: Heat oven to 350 degrees F Divide tortillas between two large pieces of foil, wrap, and warm in oven for 15 min.

Meanwhile, heat a grill pan over medium-high heat. Slice 3/4 of the onion into 1/2 in thick rounds. Finely chop remaining 1/4 onion and set aside. Toss sliced onion and peppers with 1/2 Tbsp oil and 1/4 tsp each salt and pepper. Grill until lightly charred and tender,5 to 6 min. per side. Transfer to a cutting board and thinly slice. Transfer to a large bowl and toss with corn and cheese.

To make pumpkin seed salsa, in a food processor or blender, pulse cilantro, jalapeño, Sugar, turmeric, all but 2 Tbsp. seeds, 2 Tbsp lime juice, and 1/4 tsp salt until smooth (add water, 1 Tbsp at a time, as necessary until it reaches a pesto-like consistency).

To make tomato salsa, in a medium bowl combine tomato, reserved chopped onion, remaining 2 Tbsp lime juice, and a pinch each salt and pepper.

Spread each tortilla with 1 Tbsp pumpkin seed salsa and top with vegetables (about 1/2 cup each). Roll up and place seed side down to keep closed.

Heat a large nonstick skillet over medium-high heat. Working in two batches, add 1 Tbsp oil, then cook enchiladas, seed side down first, until golden brown, about 2 min. per side. Repeat with remaining Tbsp oil and enchiladas. Serve with tomato salsa, pumpkin seed salsa, and reserved pumpkin seeds.

Per Serving 461 Cal, 22 G Fat (4.5 G SAT), 19 MG CHOL, 796 MG SOD, 19 G PRO, 48 G CARB, 6 G FIBER

Receta y escritura por Veronica Mora Vera (Mexico City)

1 Colosenses 1: 6 Que ha llegado hasta vosotros, asi como a todo el mundo, y lleva fruto y crece también en vosotros, desde el dia que oísteis y conociesteis la gracia de Dios en verdad. 1 Colosenses 1:10 para que andéis como es digno del Senor; agradándole en todo, llevando fruto en toda buena obra, y creciendo en el conocimiento de su voluntad en toda sabiduría e inteligencia espiritual.

ROLLITOS DE CARNE RELLENOS EN SALSA VERDE

Poner a freir 8 tomates verdes con cebolla, ajo, sal y pimienta. Agregar agua o caldo de pollo, una vez cocidos, se muelen en la licuadora y se pone a freir la salsa en un sarten con un poco de aceite (reservarla)

En otro sarten se ponen a freir champiñones, una lata de elote desgranado amarillo, cebolla finamente picada, ajo, 2 chiles poblanos desvenados y cortados en tiras muy delgadas hasta que esten bien cocidos y sazonados con sal y pimienta se deja enfriar en bisteces crudos se pone el relleno y se cierran con palillos de madera, se ponen a freir en sarten con aceite, voltear de ambos lados y al final se pone queso oazaca o manchego hasta derretirse. Se serven y se pone la salsa verde encima, se puede acompañar de arroz.

Receta y escritura de: Steve and Jennyfer Hopkins (Loreto Baja California Sur)

Phillipians 4:13 I can do all this through him who gives me strength.

BUCATINI ALLÁMATRICIANA

Ingredients

5 ounces bucatini pasta
1/4 cup extra – virgin olive oil 3 each crushed garlic cloves
1 1/2 ounces guanciale (cured pork cheek) sliced
¼ cup sliced red onion
1 pinch red pepper flakes
1/2 (8 ounce) can crushed San Marzano tomatoes Salt and ground back pepper to taste
1 ounce freshly grated Pecorino Romano cheese

Directions

Step 1: Fill a large pot with lightly salted water and bring to a Rolling boil. Stir in bucatini and return to a boil. Cook, uncovered, stirring occasionally, until bucatini is tender, about 11 minutes, Drain

Step 2: Heat oil in a large skillet over medium – high heat. Add garlic cloves; cook until golden brown, about 1 minute. Remove with a slotted spoon and discard. Add guanciale; cook and stir until crisp and Golden, about 4 minutes. Add onion and red pepper flakes; cook and stir until onion is translucent, about 3 minutes. Stir in tomatoes, salt, and black pepper. Simmer tomato sauce until flavors combine, about 10 minutes.

Step 3: Stir bucatin and Pecorino Romano cheese into tomato sauce and toss until evenly coated.

Recetas de : Ana Maria Morales Garcia (Cuidad de Mexico)

SOPA DE SETAS

Ingredientes

½ k de setas cortadas entrozos
1/4 cebolla rebanada
1 rama de espazote Consome de vegetables
1 rama de espazote

Preparacion

Las setas se cosen a fuego lento con un poco de agua. Cuando esten cocidasse le agrega la cebolla y cuando se les haya consumido el agua se le agrega 1 cucharada de aceite de aguacate.y se frie hasta que la cebolla este. Acitronada luego se agrega el consome de vegetales y cuando este herviendose le pone la rama de epazote. Se deja hervir por 20 min. y se sirve.

Receta de: Lau Garcia (San Miguel Allende)

SOLE MIO Boutique

Joyeria (bisuteria accesorios por línea) en Facebook tel: 415 103 3123

PASTA PRIMAVERA

Se sofríe cebolla y ajo después se agrega calabaza betabel pimiento morron en tiras delgadas en varios colores dejandolos al dente , se agrega pasta fusil cocida aderezada con sal y mantequilla y a oregano …Se combina todo para que la pasta agarre tono betabel y listo.

Receta y escritura de: Yvan Orellana (Dakota)

Proverbs 10:4 A slack hand causes poverty, but the hand of the diligent makes rich.

KNOEPHLA SOUP (German soup well known in Dakota)

Soup

1/2 cup butter
3 potatoes (peeled) cooked
1 teaspoon black pepper
3 cups milk
6 cups water
2 tablespoon chicken bouillon KNOEPHLA
1 ½ cups flour
7 tablespoons milk, or more as needed
1 egg beaten
2 teaspoons parsley
1 teaspoon black pepper
1/2 salt

Directions

Step 1 Melt butter ina large skillet over medium heat; saute potatoes, onion, and 1 ½ teaspoons black pepper until just tender, about 20 min. Stir 3 cups milk into potato mixture and heat until almost boiling, about 5 min. Remove skillet from heat.

Step 2 Bring water and chicken bouillon to a bouillon to ab boil in a Dutch oven or heavy pot.

Step 3 Combine flour, 7 tablespoons milk, egg, dill, parsley, 1 teaspoon pepper, and salt together in a bowl until dough is stiff. Add more milk, 1 tablespoon at a time, if needed. Roll dough into ropes about ½ -inch thick on a work Surface. Cut ropes into ¼ inch pieces and drop into boiling broth. Reduce heat. Cover Dutch oven with a lid, and simmer until knoephla begin to float, about 10 min.

Step 4 Stir potatoes mixture into broth and knoephla; simmer until potatoes are tender, about 20 min.

Recta y escritura de: Yvan Orellana (Dakota)

2 Timothy 1:7 For God did not give us a spirit of timidity, but a Spirit of power, of love and of self-discipline.

TACOS DE COCHINITA PIBIL

Ingredientes

1 kg de maciza de cerdo
1 taza de jugo de naranja
1 cubo de achiote
3 chiles guajillo hidratados
1 taza de vinagre de manzana
1 cda. De oregano
1 cda. De hojas de laurel seco
1 cebolla morada fileteada
1/2 taza de hojas de cilantro
4 limones
3 chiles habaneros en rodajas

Instrucciones

1. Licua el jugo, achiote, guajillo, vinagre, oregano, laurel y salpimienta. Vierte las salsa sobre la carne en una olla expres y cosela durante 30 min. Mezcla la cebolla, chile, vinagre y oregano en un tazon. Sirve la cochinita en tacos, acompaña con la cebolla de manzanos y termina con hojas de cilantro.

Recta de: Barbara Orduña Sanchez (Mineral de Pozos)

POZOLE MEXICANO

Esta preparación es para 5 personas de muy buen diente

Ingredientes:

1 kilo de amor y dedicación para que el pozole quede mas rico (es el ingrediente mas importante)
1 kilo de maíz pozolero descabezado
1 cabeza de ajo entera
1 3/4 de lomo o de pierna de puerco
400 gramos de patitas de purerco bien limpias
1 cebolla partida a la mitad para cocer las carnes Sal a gusto
6 chiles anchos desvenados, despepitados y remojados en agua mu caliente
1 cucharada de oregano-Caldo donde se cocieron las carnes, el necesario
Nota: La crne de cerdo la puedes reemplazar por pollo si asi lo prefieres.
2 lechugas orejonas medianas en rebanadas delgadas
1 manojo de rabanitos bien lavados y rebanados
2 cebollas medianas finamente picadas Limones partidos en cuarterones
16 toastadas
Salsa picosa
Ingredientes para la salsa picosa
20 chiles de árbol asados 1" taza de vinagre
Sal al gusto

Preparacion:

El maíz se enjuaga muy bien y se descabeza (porque de no hacerlo no florea) y se pone a cocer a cubrir y sin sal hasta que este suave

Las carnes se ponen a cocer aparte con la cebolla y la sal, y cuando este suaves se parten en trozos, las patitas se deshusesany se parten en trozos.

Los chiles anchos se muelen con su agua de remojo y el oregano y se cuelan en la olla donde están los granos de maíz. Ahí se agrega la carne y un poco del caldo donde se cocio: se sazona con sal y se deja hervir todo junto durante 15 minutos.

El caldo de pozole debe quedar como un atole muy ligero

Se retira la cabeza de ajo y se sirve muy caliente acompañado del resto
Preparacion de la salsa picos

Se muelen todos los ingredientes.
Como servir el pozole

Se presenta en una olla de barro y se sirve en tazoncitos también de barro, de los llamado "pozoleros

" Aparte se pone el resto de los ingredientes en platitios separados o en un platon de barro que tenga divisiones. La salsa picante se sirve en una cazuelita por separado.

Receta y frase de: Olivia Martinez (San Miguel Allende)

Frase: Be Alone
Eat alone, take yourself on dates, sleep alone. In the midst of this you will learn about yourself. You will grow, you will figure out what inspires you, you will curate your own dreams, your own beliefs, your own stunning clarity, and when you do meet the person who makes your cells dance, you will be sure of it, because you are sure of yourself.

TAQUITOS DE FRIJO CON CARNE DE PUERCO

Ingredientes:

1/4 kg. Maciza de puerco
3 Papas medianas cocidas
10 tortillas
1 Taza de frijol cocido sin caldo Chipotle de lata al gusto
Sal al gusto
Crema Queso

Preparacion:

Se cuece la carne con sal y agua, puede se en uan olla de presión. Se ponen los frijoles y las papas en una cacerola con un poco de caldo de la carne, se aplastan hasta hacer un pure, se aplastan hasta hacer un pure, se agrega la carne deshervada ya cocida y los chipotles en pedacitos, se mezcla todo muy bien , se deja hervir hasta que espese y con esto se rellenan las tortillas y se forman los taquitos, se fríen y se sirven con **crema y queso**.

Receta de: Alma Haydee (Cuidad de Mexico)

CREPAS TIPO MAMY JULY (receta de mama de Alma)

Ingredientes:

Tortillas de harina
Jamon de pavo
Salsa para espaguetis
Cebolla
Mantequilla
Crema y queso manchego rayado

Preparacion :

Con las tortillas se hacen unos tacos rellenos del jamon, acomodarlos en un refractario. En una olla se frie con la mantequilla la cebolla fileteada (1/4 y salsa (de bote ya preparada a la boloñesa)se sazonar con

un poco de consome . Banar las crepas del refractario y colocar la crema y meter al horno para gratinar. Mmmmmm a disfrutarlo!!!

Receta de: Silvia Diaz (Cuidad de Mexico)

Colosenses 3:16-17 Que el mensaje de Cristo , con toda su riqueza, llene sus vidas. Ensenense y aconséjense unos a otros con toda la sabiduría que el da. Canten salmos e himnos canciones espirituales a Dios con un corazón agradecido. Y todo lo que hagan o digan, haganlo como representantes del Senor Jesus y den gracias a Dios Padre por medio de el.

PECHUGAS DE POLLO EN SALSA POBLANA

Ingredientes:

(para cuarto personas tragonas)

2 pechugas cocidas con sal ajo y cebolla y partidas en medallones 200 ml
de crema acida

5 chiles poblanos grandes asados pelados y desvenados 1/2
cdita de sal

cda de mantequilla

1 taza de queso manchego rallado

Procedimiento:

Se licua la crema, 4 chiles y la sal y se sazona en un sarten con la mantequilla Unte
con esta mezcla el fondo de un refractario

Coloque el pollo y cúbralo con el resto de la preparación
EspoLvoree por encima con el queso

El chile que no licuo cortelo en rajas pequeñas

Y adorne con este el plato

Hornea a 190 grado C hasta que gratine o hasta que la salsa hierva

Si lo prefiere cueza con la flama muy bajita utilizando una cacerola en lugar de refractario y ya para servir espolvorear el queso y las rajitas sobre el plato.

Receta de: Coco (San Miguel Allende)

POZOLE BLANCO

1 kg. De maíz precocido 1 k de codillo de puerco 1 k de cabeza de puerco
En olla express se pone suficiente agua, con sal, se le agrega el maíz y la carne.
Se prepara en un lienzo limpio 1 cebolla 1 cabeza de ajo, tomillo, laurel, mejorana (yerbas de olor)
Y se amarra para que no nade en el caldo, solo que salga su sabor. Se deja cocer por una hora y media
Se pica lechuga, cebolla, rabanitos se espovorea oregano y se le pone limon.
Salsa Picosa para Pozole
10 chiles morita o de árbol fritos 1 cabeza de ajos fritos
1 cuch. de oregano , sal media tasa de vinagre   media tasa de agua

Para la salsa se licuan los chiles dorados en aciete con los ajos también dorados en aceite se le agrega el viangre y el agua y la cucharada de oregano . Sal a gusto.

Se sirve el caldo con el maíz, la carne deshebrada y se le agrega lechuga, cebolla picada, rabanitos cortados en rodajas, oregano y tostadas con crema y queso cotija rallado para acompañar el rico pozole.

Bon Apetit!

Receta de: Doctora Yvonne Assam (5522713839) (Cuidad de Mexico)

Ejercita el corazón y tonifica el alma

PASTEL AZTECA CON CHILE POBLANO

Tortillas de fríen se ponen en el refractario se muele una bolsa de chiles poblanos con medio litro de crema ajo cebolla un trozo y 150 gramos de queso manchego. La pechuga de pollo se deshereda y se pone una capa de tortilla una de salsa una de pollo y asi hasta completar hasta arriba el refractario y a lo ultimo se pone queso manchego y se hornea. Se sirve con frijoles refritos.

Recta de: Baltasar Portillo (San Miguel Allende)

PEA, SCALLIONOPN, AND GRUYERE QUICHE

Ingredients

19 inch refrigerated rolled pie crust (from a 15 – ounce package)
4 ounces Gruyere, grated (about 1 cup)
4 large eggs, lightly beaten
2 cups half and half
¾ cup frozen peas
2 scallions, sliced
Kosher salt and black pepper green salad, for serving

How to Make It

Step 1
Heat oven to 375 F with the rack in the lowest position. Press the pie crust into a 9 inch pie plate. Sprinkle the bottom with the cheese.

Step 2 Whisk together the eggs, half and half , peas, scallions, 3/4 teaspoon salt, and 1/4 teaspoon pepper. Pour the mixture in the piecrust. Bake until the crust is golden brown and the filling is set, 50 to 55 min. Let rest for 5 minutes before serving.

Step 3

Serve the quiche warm or at room temperature with the salad.

Receta de: Olivia Martinez (San Miguel Allende)

HAMBURGUESA VEGETARIANAS

Hamburguesa:

250 Gr de lentejas
1 huevo
1 ajo
1/4 de cebolla
Salsa inglesa C/N
Cilantro C/N y Sal

Mayonesa:

1 taza de mayonesa
Cilantro C/N
1 ajo

Se remojan toda la noche las lentejas, se muelen en un procesador con todos los demás ingredientes, se forman las hamburguesas y se fríen, se acompañan con la mayonesa de cilantro y ajo. Esta se hace licuando la mayonesa con el ajo y el cilantro. Puedes ponerlas en bollos y ponerle lechuga, jitomate, cebolla rebanada, cátsup, mostaza o lo que gustes.

Quedan muy ricas!

Receta de: ***Guadalupe Machuca***

PESCADO ENVINADO

6 rodajas de pescado
1 vaso de vino blanco
2 cucharadas soperas de perejil bien picado
6 trocitos de margarina
3 dientes de ajo picaditos Sal y pimienta al gusto

Procedimiento:

1. Lavar el pescado, secarlo y espolvorearlo con sal y pimienta y se coloca en un recipiente refractario
2. Banarlas rodajas con el vino y colocar encima el ajo, el perejil y trocitos de margarina
3. Horneara fuego medio durante 20 min. Bañando de vez en cuando con un poco de vino.

Buen Provecho

Receta de: Maribel Mora Estrella Voluntaria en Asilo Alma (San Miguel Allende)

LENTEJAS MARIBEL

Para 6 personas

Ingredientes:

  1/4 de lentejas Cebolla
  Ajo y sal algusto
  1/4 carne de puerco en trozos
  1/4 chorizo
  1/4 tocino 3 tomates

Preparacion:

Pones a cocer las lentejas, cebolla, ajo, sal (20 min.)

El otro sarten pones a cocer la carne de puerco en tozos con poco de agua 15 min. Poner sal agusto Sacas la carne de puerco y la pones el un recipiente, poner el chorizo y el tocino y freir juntos. Molier el tomate en la liquadora con ajo y comino, cebolla. Vaciar donde esta la carne de puerco , chorizo y tocino. Remover y ultimo agregar las lentejas. Y Listo.

Receta de: Lourdes Bucio dar clases de manejo de maquina de coser, Patchwork, bordado, macramé y mas cosas. @a2manossma tel. 3318508623 (San Miguel Allende)

CARNE EN SU JUGO

Ingredientes:

1 kg de carne muy jugosa que se pedirá que sea rebanada muy delgada (en Guadalajara la rebanan en rebanadora) y picada my finita.
1/4 tocino rebanado igual muy fino.
1/4 tomatillo
Cilantro y sazonador

Para el caldo:

Poner a hervir un hueso poroso, una papa y una zanahoria sin pelar, un puño de cilantro, ajo y cebolla. Cuando el hueso saque lo café, retirar del caldo y añadir jitomate molido y sal. Dejar hervir. Reservar.

Procedimineto:

Poner a freir el tocino, ahí añadir la carne picada y dejar tapada para que saque el jugo. Mover Cuando veas que ya solto el jugo añadir el tomatillo molido con un poco de caldo el puño de cilantro y sazonador. Dejar hervir y cubrir con el resto del caldo colado.

Para servir: Tener frijoles de la olla. Y poner en plato hondo la carne en su jugo muy caliente y frijoles. En la mesa tener cilantro, chile serrano, jitomate y cebolla picada para que se le añada y limon. Y acompañar con tostadas o tortillas.

Recta y 3 escrituras: Adriana Gilbert Hurtado (San Miguel Allende)

Genesis 9:3 "Todo lo que se mueve y vivie, os será para mantenimiento: asi como las legumbres y plantas verdes, os lo he dado todo."

Genesis 1:29 Tambien les dijo: Yo les doy de la tierra todas las plantas que producen semilla; todo esto les servirá de alimento.

Nehemias 8:10 Luego Nehemias añadió: Ya pueden irse. Coman bien, tomen bebidas dulces y compartan su comida con quienes no tengan nada, porque este dia he sido consagrado a nuestro Señor es nuestra fortaleza

POLLO AL EPAZOTE (es una receta de la Sierra Tarahumara)

Ingredientes:

Chile Sierrano seco lo que les guste de picoso.
1 diente de ajo
1 trozo de canela
2 clavos
2 elotes troceados en 3
1 mango de epazote
Un poco de aceite
4 jitomates (se parten 4)

Preparacion:

Tanto los jitomates, chiles, un poco de epazote ye el diente de ajo se fríen en aceite para después licuarlos con los clavos y la canel que desees.

En una cacerola agrega los elotes, se incorpora lo licuado y deja hervir por 10 minutos.

Despues agrega el pollo a fuego lento y tapalo por 20 minutos o hasta que se cueza agrega las demás ramas de epazote y sal a gusto. Y disfrutalo

Recipe and scripture by: Sherry Comes (Colorado)

1 Corinthians 16:15 " Do everything in love "

If you're on the go, peanut butter and jelly can be your meal of choice.

TRADITIONAL PEANUT BUTTER AND JELLY

Ingredients

  2 slices sandwich bread (or toasted)
  2 tablespoons peanut butter (or amount as you wish)
  2 teaspoons strawberry jam (or amount as you wish)

Directions:

Spread the peanut butter on one piece of bread together to form a sandwich.

Notes:

Notes:

Recetas de Familia Obregon

2 Recetas y Frase de Irma Obegon Pintora (Valle de Bravo)

Ama se Luz y Haz la diferencia en Este Mundo

1 Receta: BOTONAS DE JOCOQUE DELI

Ingredientes

Jocoque seco uvas moradas , Cebolla, Chile serrano, Nuez , Blue Cheese

Modod de preparación: Picas todos los ingredientes en trozos muy chiquitos y los mezclas. El Blue cheese va desmoronado, pero la cantidad va depender de que tanto te guste el sabor (Yo le pongo la mitad de uno de 100g.) Al final le agregas sal aceite de oliva.

2nd Receta: PESCADO DELICIOSO

En una ollita poner aceite de olivo, jitomate sen semilla cortado en cuadritos y albahaca picadita , mantener caliente. Salpimentar filete de pescado y asarlo en un sarten de telon. Bañar con la mezcla caliente que se había preparado antes. Es muy sencillo pero buenisimo!

Receta y frase de: Dany Lascurain de Oyanguren (Cuidad de Mexico)

Suelta lo que pesa, Ama lo que tienes, Agradece lo que llega

ENSALADA DE PORTIBELLO

Portibello rebanado a lo largo (como si fuera carpaccio) y lo dejas marinando mínimo una hra con aceite, vinagre balsamico, sal gruesa y pimeienta. A eso le agregas pediazitos de jitomate deshidratado y queso de cabra.

Receta y escritura de: Fernanada de Lascurain (Boston)

Proverbs: 16:24 Panal de miel son los dichos suaves; suavidad al alma y medicina para los huesos

BOWEL DE ATUN

Ingredientes

1/4 taza de arroz al vapor 1/4 taza Zanahoria rallada 1/2 pepino rebanado
1 rabano
Un punito de espinaca Ajonjoli tostado
50 gr de lomo de atun congelado

Modo de preparación

Poner el arroz a cocer 1/4 de taza por 1/2 taza de agua

Mientras tanto rallar la zanahoria, rebanar el pepino y el rabano.

Cortar el lomo de atun en cuadros

Marinar con el jugo de dos limones, 1/2 cucharadita de vinagre de arroz, 1 cucharadita de ponzu o salsa de soya, 1 cucharadita de aceite de ajonjolí…mezclar bien y dejar en el refrigerador en lo que se hace el arroz.

En un bowl colocar el arroz, encima vamos a dividir nuestro bowl en 4 partes en el primer cuadrante colocamos la zanahoria,después el rabano, la espinaca, el pepino y finalmente el atun.

Podemos decorar con un poco de algas troceadas y espolvorear con ajonjolí tostado y listo!

Puedes agregarle al atun cebolla morada o cebollin para darle un toque mas de sabor y se me olvidaba jengibre ralllado

Receta de Ximana De Lascurain   @tippingmexico Rentar casa Increibles (Cuidad de Mexico)

No Esperes Que La luz del Destino Ilumine tu Vidad, Iluminala Tu

SOPA DE CEBOLLA

Ingredientes:

1 cebolla rebanada en plumitas
Mantequilla

2 latas de caldo de Rea Campbell's Pan
baguette duro

Queso gruyere

2 cdas de salsa maggi

Modo de preparación: Sofrie la cebolla con mantequilla y aceite hasta que quede transparente. Agregar las 2 latas de caldo de res y la misma medida de agua . Sazonar con Knor Suiza y poca sal. Siempre probar para checar el sazon. Cortar la baguette en cuadros pequeños y meter al horno para tostar. Servir bien caliente, agregar los trozos de pan y queso encima. Arriba 2 latas caldo de res.

Receta de Carla Lascurain (Cuidad de Mexico)

"Si no esta en tus manos cambiar una situación que te produce dolor, siempre podras escoger la actitud con la que afrontes ese sufrimiento."

PESCADO RODRIGO

Ingredientes

10 filetes de pescado
blanco Salsa Maggie

Salsa
Inglesa
Vinagre
balsamico
Limon

Aciete de oliva , Chile serrano picado finito , Cebolla y cilantro finamente picados

Modo de preparación:

Poner los pescados marinar con las salsas y el vinagre balsamico. Ponerlos a la plancha y desmenuzarlos. Agregar un chirrido de aceite de oliva, mas salsa Maggie, Inglesa y acete balsamico. Incorporar el chile, la cebolla, el cilantro y el jugo de algunos limones. Revolver y servir Listo!

Receta y Frase de Tere Obregon Diseñadira (Cuidad de Mexico)

Siempre Natural y Sencilla

ENSALADA DE VERDOLAGA

1 Kilo de verdolaga (las puras hojas)
2 toronjas en gajos
1 aguacate partido en gajos
1 cebolla morada (rebanadas muy delgadas)
1 lata de col fermentada (la venden en la europea)
Vinagreta: aceite y vinagre y Sal y Pimienta

3 Recetas y Frase de : Santiago Cortina Obregon Arquitecto y Chef (Cuidad de Mexico)

No hay mas excusas, ponte el delantal y anímate a cocinar.

1 receta : SASHIMI DE ROBALO CON AJO QUEMADO

4 Porciones aproximadamente 1 lonja de robalo de 300 gramos
3 dientes de ajo , 2 limones amarilos , 2 cucharadas de ponzu , 1 cucharada de aceite de olivo
2 cucharaditas de ajonjolí negro, 1 chucharadita de ralaldura de limon , 1 chile hebanero

2nd Receta

TATAKI DE PICAÑA

Primero vamos a preparar un mantequilla con las cucharadas de queso azul, sal y pimienta. Se la untamos a la picaña y la vamos a sellar en la parrilla o en el sarten.

La sellamos unos 4-5 min. de cada lado y la vamos a cortar en lajas como de ½ cm de espesor. Lo colocamos en un plato y vamos a preparar un salsa con el perejil finamente picado, aceite de olivo, mostaza y el jugo de los limones. Se lo vertimos a las laminas de picaña, y espolvoreamos queso parmesano y Listo!

3rd Recta: CALLOS DE HATCHA CON SALSA TABBOU

Primero vamos a pelar el pepino, y lo vamos a cortar en cuadros pequeños junto con el tomate rojo y la cebolla morada. Picar finamente los dientes de ajo . En un tazon vamos a poner la verdura, el jugo de limon amarillo y su ralladura junto con la de jengibre. El aceite de olivo, la salsa ponzu y el aceite de ajonjolí. Sal y pimienta.

Ya quqe este preparada la salsa vamos a poner los callos de hacha en un sarten a que se doren poco, con un chorrito de aceite de olivo, sal y pimienta. Servimos en un plato, primero las verduras y encima ponemos los callos y listo.

Callos de Hatcha con salsa TABBOU

Tataki de Picaña

Sashimi de Robalo con ajo quemado

Receta de: Eugenia Trevino (Cuidad de Mexico)

Tienes dos cartas: El No ya lo tienes, ve por el si

CHILES RELLENOS (mi mama)
8 Chiles poblanos
1/2 Kg. Queso Oaxaca, manchego o chihuahua o con frijoles
1 Cebolla
3 Tazas de agua 1/2 Taza de harina
Aceite, sal y pimienta

Modo de Hacerse

Se asan lo chiles directo a la lumbre y ya que están asados los meto en una bolsa de plástico durante 1/2 hora a que suden, se pelan (el pellejito), con un cuchillo les corto una tira y les saco las semillas. Se enjagan cuidando de no romperlos. Se ponen a escurrir.

Los relleno de bastante queso (o frijoles) y los atoro con un palillo.

En un platon pongo el harina la mezclo con la sal y a aparte una cebolla la rebano en ruedas y las pongo en un caso con aceite caliente a que esten transparentes (5 min.) ahí mismo frio los chiles enharinados y ya que esten dorados les pongo el agua hasta cubrirlos a que hiervan tapados de 15 a 20 min. A fuego lento .

Deliciosos!!! Se sirven con frijoles refritos.

Receta y escrituras de: Mary Cupido (Cuidad de Mexico)

Juan 1:12 Mas a todos los que le recibieron, a los que creen en su nombre, les dio potestad de ser hechos hijos de Dios. Filipenses 4:19 Mi Dios, pues, suplirá todo lo que os falta conforme a sus riquezas en gloria en Cristo Jesus.

CREMA DE CILANTRO

Ingredientes:

1 manojo de cilantro
1 papa
1 diente de ajo
1 trozo de cebolla
1 queso Philadelphia de 90 grs.
1 cucharadita de consome
Crutones al gusto
Modo de preparación:
En una olla se ponen a cocer el cilantro, la papa (con todo y cascara)
El ajo y la cebolla

En la licuadora se colocan todos los ingredientes ya cocidos junto con el queso Philadelphia y el consome.

Ya que todo este bien molido, se vuelve a poner en la olla, se le pone un poco mas de agua y se deja jervir unos min., cuidando de que no se derrame. Se sirve en platos soperos y se le agregan crutones al gusto.

Rinde de 4 a 6 porciones.

Receta y frase de: Olivia Martinez (San Miguel Allende)

Comence a ser libre Cuando descubri que la Jaula estaba Hecha de Pensamientos.

SOPA DE CILANTRO

Ingredientes:

1 Manojo de cilantro
1 queso crema
1 1/2 de caldo de pollo
1 diente de ajo
1/4 de cebolla
Sal y pimienta

Preparación

Acitronar el ajo y la cebolla licuar con el resto de los ingredientes con un poco de el caldo de pollo, colar, ponerlo en una cacerola a calentar y agregar el resto del caldo de pollo.

Receta de: Ofelia Garcia Monroy (Cuidad de Mexico)

NOPALES CON CURCUMA

Ingredientes:

Nopales medianos cortados en trozos
1 Papa en cuadritos
1/2 taza de poro rebanado
1 taza de jtomate picado
1/2 taza de cilantro picado
1 cucharadita de curuma

Preparacion:

Se cocen los noales se escurren

Y se enjuagan para quitarles la baba

En una cacerola se frie el poro cuando este acitronado se agrega el jitomate picado y la papa en trozos. Se le pone agua y cuando este cocida las papas. Se le agregan los nopales y cuando este hirviendo se le agrega la cucharadita de curcuma y el cilantro, sal al gusto sedeja hervir unos 20 min. y se sirve.

Recipe and scriptures by: Angelica Maria Thompson Teacher (Smyrna)

Jeremiah 15:16 Your words were found , and I ate them, and your word was to me the joy and rejoicing of my heart; For I am called by your name, O LORD God of hosts.

CHICKEN QUESADILLAS

Ingredients

3 whole boneless, skinless chicken breasts
2 tbsp. Taco or Tex-Mex seasoning
Vegetable or Olive Oil for frying
1 whole large onion
1 whole large bell pepper (color of your choice)
12 whole small flour tortillas (fajita size)
2 1/2 c. grated cheddar Jack Cheese (or straight Jack)
Hot sauce (I used cholula)
Butter for frying Salsa, for serving
Sour cream, for serving
Cilantro for serving
Jalapeño slices, for serving

Directions:

Heat vegetable oil or olive oil in a skillet over high heat. Sprinkle both sides of the chicken with taco seasoning. Add the chicken to the skills and saute over medium-high heat until done, about 4 min. per side. Remove fro the skillet, allow to cool slightly, and dice into cubes. Set aside.

In the same skillet over medium-high heat, throw in the onions and peppers and cook until the veggies are golden brown, 3 to 4 min. Remove from the skillet, allow to cool slightly, and dice into cubes. Set aside.

Melt 1/2 tablespoon of the butter in a separate skillet or griddle over medium heat and lay a flour tortilla in the skillet. Build the quesadillas by laying a good amount of grated cheese on the bottom tortilla, and then arranging the chicken and cooked peppers on the cheese. Top with a little more grated cheese and top with a second tortilla. When the tortilla is golden on the first side, carefully flip the quesadilla to the other side, adding another 1/2 tablespoon butter to the skillet at the same time. Continue cooking until the second side is golden.

Repeat with the remaining tortilla and fillings. Cut into wedges and serve with salsa, sour cream, jalapeño slices, and cilantro.

Receta de: Karin Olguin: Broker Inmobiliario Lum Inmobiliaria 5548 36 4803 Cuidad de Mexico

Receta De La Birria Mexicana

Ingredientes:

1 1/2 kg. Carne falda de res.
8 chiles guajillo
4 tomates
1/2 cebolla
5 dientes de ajo
2 1/2 litros de agua
Especias al gusto
45 pimientas
1/2 cucharita de comino
1 cucharada de oregano
5 clavos de olor
5 hojas de laurel
1/4 cucharadita de sal de ajo
Cilantro al gusto
1 cebolla morada

Preparacion:

Recomiendo para que sea as rápido utilizar olla express. Pon en la olla express a cocer 1 1/2 kg. De carne de falda de res en dos litros de agua, de preferencia agregar hueso con tuétano para darle mas sabor a la birria.

Licuar los 9 chiles guajuillo previamente hidratados sin semillas incorpora el ajo, cebolla y especias y vaciar sin colar en la carne una vez que ya este bien cocina aprox. Unos 45 min. Incorporalo, agrega tres piscas de especias surtidas y dejalo cocer por 20 min. mas y listo.

Sirves con cilantro picado, limon y para acompañado de una tortillas hechas a mano y a disfrutar.

Receta y escritura de: Anne De Garcia (San Miguel Allende)

Hechos 2:46-47 2 Y perseverando unánimes cada dia en el templo, y partiendo el pan en las casa, comían juntos con alegría y sencillez de corazón, alabando a Dios, y teniendo favor con todo el pueblo. Y el Señor añadia cada dia a la iglesia los que habían de ser salvos."

POLLO EN SALSA DE CILANTRO

Ingredientes:

1 pechuga de pollo grande
1 manojo de cilantro
1 lata de carnetion
1 lata de media crema
1/2 barra de queso philadelphia
2 cubitos de consome de pollo
1/2 taza de caldo de pollo que cocimos
2 cucharadas de mantequilla
2 cucharadas de mantequilla

Preparacion:

Vamos a cocer la pechuga de pollo y una vez lista la desmenuzamos.

Para preparar la salsa:

En la licuadora vamos a poner el resto de los ingredientes excepto la mantequilla, y vamos a licuar hasta que este todo bien mezclado.

En una cacerola vamos a poner las dos cucharadas de mantequilla, y vamos a saltear el pollo unos minutos. Añadimos la salsa y dejamos que hierva cinco minutos mas mezclándola con el pollo y moviendo para que no se pegue. Y listo, disfrutalo con tortillas de harina, de maíz o pan de caja. Dios te bendiga

Notes:

Notes:

Side Dishes

ARGENTINE CHIMICHURRI

Ingredients:

6 T olive oil
2 T red wine vinegar
1 large handful flat-leaf parsley finely Chopped (about 1/3 Cup loosely packed)
1 T fresh thyme
leaves finely chopped
1 teaspoon toasted cumin
Optional juice of ½ lemon
½ teaspoon red chili flakes
1 clove garlic, peeled and crushed but left whole Salt and pepper to taste

Instructions:

Combine all ingredients in a jar with a lid. Shake vigorously.

Taste and adjust seasoning.

Let chimichurri sit while dinner is prepared to flavors meld.

Recipe by Reverend Canon George F. Woodward III Rector St. Paul's Church (SMA)

MASHED POTATO CASSEROLE

Serves 10

Ingredients:

4lbs. (12) potatoes
1 package (8 oz.) of cream cheese, softened
1 Cup Sour Cream
2 teaspoons salt
1/8 teaspoon pepper
1 clove crushed garlic (or two or three Garlic to taste)
¼ Cup chopped chives
½ teaspoon paprika
1 Tablespoon butter

Instructions:

Cook potatoes, drain and mash.

Add cheese, sour cream, garlic, salt and pepper.
Beat at high speed.

Stir in chopped chives.

Spoon into greased 10 cup baking
dish Sprinkle with paprika.

Dot with butter.

Bake 30 minutes at 350 degrees.

May be made ahead and refrigerated. If so, let stand to room temp before baking, or plan to bake longer (40 minutes)

Recipe by Reverend Canon George F. Woodward III Rector St. Paul's Church (SMA)

YELLOW BEET SALAD WITH MUSTARD SEED DRESSING

Ingredients:

5 or 6 medium yellow beets (2 lbs.)
1 shallot finely diced
2 tablespoons lemon juice
1 Tablespoon rice vinegar
1 teaspoon Dijon mustard
2 Tablespoons freshly grated horseradish (and more for garnish)
Salt and Pepper
4 tablespoons mild vegetable oil
1 Teaspoon black mustard seeds
½ teaspoon nigella seeds (optional)

Instructions:

Heat over to 375 and put scrubbed beets in small roasting pan with an inch of water in the bottom. Cover tightly and bake until beets are tender to the knife…about 1hour.

Make the vinaigrette: Shallot, lemon juice, rice vinegar, mustard and horseradish in a bowl. Pinch of salt and pepper. Whisk in 3 Tablespoons of vegetable oil.

Heat a small skillet with 1 Tablespoon of oil. Add mustard seeds and nigella seeds. They will begin in pop after 1 minute. Scrape seeds and oil into vinaigrette.

Let beets cool slightly then rub off skin. Slice beets crosswise into quarter inch rounds and place in salad bowl.

Sprinkle beets lightly with salt, toss with dressing, serve garnished with horseradish and serve at room temp.

(I have skipped the nigella seeds until I figure out what they are, and didn't heat the mustard seeds and all was dandy).

Recipe by Lynn Ramsey St. Paul's Church Despensa Project (San Miguel de Allende)

ASHVILLE CHEESE SALAD

Ingredients:

1 can tomato soup
7 oz. pkg cream cheese Tbsp. Unflavored gelatin
8 1 c. mayonnaise
1 ½ c. mixture of chopped celery, green olives, green pepper and onion

Instructions:

Heat soup, then stir in cream cheese until smooth.

Add gelatin which has been softened in cold water.
Cool. Add other ingredients.

Place in refrigerator to set.

Cut into squares to serve with dollop of may and capers to garnish.

This makes an 8x8 pan, double recipe for 9x13 pan.

Great variation: Add 1 can sockeye salmon, double the gelatin, and add chopped dill pickle to mixture.

Recipe by Susan Gist St. Paul's Church (San Miguel de Allende)

Psalm 107: 9 - For he satisfies the thirsty and fills the hungry with good things

John 6:35 – Jesus replied, "I am the bread of life. Whoever comes to me will never be hungry again. Whoever believes in me will never be thirsty."

1 Corinthians 10: 31 So whether you eat or drink, or whatever you do, do it all for the glory of God.

TEXAS CAVIAR

Ingredients:

3 16 oz. cans black-eyed, drained and rinsed of all juice
1 small jar chopped pimentos, juice included
1 bunch scallions, thinly sliced, green part only
1 Tablespoon fresh oregano or 1 tsp. dried oregano leaves
1 Tablespoon Tabasco sauce
1 Tablespoon Worcestershire sauce
1 teaspoon black pepper
½ teaspoon black pepper
½ bunch parsley or cilantro, chopped
3 canned or fresh jalapeño chilies, chopped
1 firm, ripe chopped tomato or 1 can Ro-Tel tomatoes
½ Cup olive oil + ¼ Cup balsamic vinegar
1 green bell pepper, finely chopped
3 cloves fresh garlic, pressed or minced

Instructions:

In a large bowl, stir all ingredients very well.

Refrigerate for at least 4-6 hours, preferably overnight, in a sealed or covered container.
Remember the longer it sits, the better it gets!

Service with old-fashioned saltine crackers or with corn tortilla chips.

Recipe by Jenny Kersten St. Paul's Church (San Miguel de Allende)

OLIVE CHEESE NUGGETS

Yield 12 servings

Ingredients:

1 cup (4 ounces) shredded sharp Cheddar cheese
¼ cup (½ stick) margarine, softened
¾ cup sifted flour
1/8 teaspoon salt
½ teaspoon paprika
¼ teaspoon cayenne pepper (optional)
35 to 40 stuffed green olives

Instructions:

Preheat the oven to 400 degrees.

Combine the cheese and margarine in a bowl and mix well.

Stir the flour, salt, paprika and cayenne pepper together, add to the cheese mixture and mix until a dough forms.

Knead on a floured surface if necessary.

Shape approximately 1 teaspoon of dough around each olive to enclose and seal completely.
Place the olives on an ungreased baking sheet.

Bake for 12 to 15 minutes or until golden brown. Serve warm or cold.

The unbaked olives may be frozen and baked as needed.

The cheese dough may be shaped into pencil – size sticks and baked as above to make crisp delicious cheese sticks

Recipe by Jenny Kersten St. Paul's Church (San Miguel de Allende)

CRANBERRY APPLE PEAR SAUCE

Ingredients:

2 pounds fresh cranberries
3 apples, pared, cored, diced
2 pears, pared, cored diced
2 cups golden raisins
2 cups sugar
1 cup fresh orange juice (about 3 oranges)
2 tablespoons grated orange peel
2 teaspoons ground cinnamon
¼ teaspoon freshly grated nutmeg
½ cup Cointreau or Orange-flavored liqueur

Instructions:

Heat all ingredients except liqueur in large saucepan to boiling; reduce heat.

Simmer uncovered, stirring frequently, until mixture thickens, about 45 minutes.

Remove from heat, stir in liqueur

Refrigerate covered 4 hours or

overnight Serve sauce slightly chilled.

Recipe and scripture by Jenny Ann Kersten St. Paul's Church (San Miguel de Allende)

1 Corinthians 10:13: No temptation has seized you except what is common to men. And God is faithful; he will not let let you be tempted beyond what you can bear. But when you are tempted, he will also provide a way out so that you can stand up under it.

CARROT AND SWEET POTATO SOUP

Ingredients:

4 Tbsp. unsalted butter
1 medium onion, chopped
2 tsp. curry powder
2 cloves garlic, copped
2 medium sweet potatoes, peeled and chopped
4 carrots. Peeled and chopped
1 apple, peeled, peeled cored and chopped
4 cups chicken broth
2 Tbps. honey
Salt and pepper to taste
Garnishes:
A dollop of yogurt or sour cream
Spring onions and / or chives, finely chopped

Instructions:

Melt butter in a large pot over medium high heat.

Add onions and cook, stirring occasionally, until translucent, about 10 minutes.
Add curry powder and cook another minute.

Add the garlic, sweet potatoes, carrots, apple, bell pepper, chicken broth, honey, salt , and pepper and bring to a boil.

Cover and simmer over low heat until vegetables are very tender.

Using a stick blender, puree the soup directly i the pot until smooth and creamy. Alternatively, cool the soup slightly then puree in a regular blender in batches and return to the pot.

Be sure to leave the hole in the lid open, and cover with a kitchen towel, to allow the steam to escape.

Taste and adjust
seasonings.

Ladle soup into bowls.

Add garnishes before serving or let your guests help themselves!

Receta de: Gabriela Abud Pintora (Cuidad de Mexico)

ENSALADA DE TABULE comida ARABE (del Mediterraneo)

Ingredientes para 4

Media taza de trigo quebrado, remojado, enjuagado y exprimido 3 o 4 cebollas cambray picadas
Un manojo de perejil (solo las hojas) lavado y picado
Medio manojo de hojas de hierbabuena (sola las hojas) picadas 3 jitomates rojos picados
Todo esto se coloca en un bowl y se anade el jugo de 2 limones, sal al gusto, poca pimienta y un buen chorro de aceite de oliva.

Se mezcla muy bien y se adorna con hojas de lechuga orejona para degustar.

Sagtain – Buen provecho

Esta ensalada puede ser una botana o para acompañar al platillo principal.

Receta de : Lic. Enfermeria y Tanatologa Jaqueline Salgado (San Miguel Allende)

PURE DE PAPA

4 papas grandes

Mantequilla

Leche

Pimienta y sal al guesto

Se cocen las papas ya tibias se machaca, en un sarten se pine un pedazo ¼ aprox. De mantequilla y se pone la papa, se va moviendo hasta que se compacte y se le agrega un poco de leche con la sal y muy piquita pimienta, se incorpora toedo hasta que queda especita y listo.

Recipe and scripture by : Sandra Orellana Writer (San Miguel Allende)

Matthew 6:11 Give us today our daily bread.

DRESSING (for Thanksgiving or Christimas)

Ingredients

1 cup chop onion 3 cups chop celery
½ butter
Cubed bread 1 loaf (toasted)
1 cup pecans
1/3 perijil
1 teaspoon poultry Chicken boubion Raisans

Saute celery, onion, pecans, perijil, and butter in a pan
Put the cube toast bread on a glass pan for oven and pour mixed ingredients and layer cubed toasted bread and repeat. Pour chicken broth until it´s moist. Put inside oven 180 degrees Fahrenheit for 20 min. If you make this a day before. The flavor is better.

Receta de: MaEsther Tapia Rosales (Tenacingo)

ARCOS DE CEBOLLA

12 porciones

Ingredientes:

4 cebollas
2 tzazas de harina
4 cucharaditas polvo hornear
4 huevos
1 taza de leche
Sal y pimienta al gusto Aceite vegetal el necesario

Preparacion:
Pelar las cebollas y cortarlas, en rebanadas de un poco mas de un centimetro de ancho y separar, los arcos.

En un tazon mezcalar y batir hasta lograr una mezcla suave la harina, polvo para hornear, huevos, leche y las sal pimienta en una sarten colocar el aceite a fuego alto, colocar los aros previamente banados con la

mezcla anterior, freírlas hasta que doren ligeramente Hecho lo anterior, en otro recipiente poner servilleta de papel para eliminar el exceso de grasa y listo para servir.

Receta de: Norma De Leon Ibarra Directora de Enlace y Headhunting (Cuidad de Mexico)

RAJAS CON CREMA:

24 chiles poblanos medianos
Media cebolla
2 cucharadas de Knorr suiza
Crema acida, de preferencia Alpura

Preparacion: 30 min.
En las hornillas de la estufa, pon a " tatemar" los chiles directamente al fuego. Cuando los chiles esten totalmente negros, guardalos en una bolsa de celofan para que, al sudar, sea mas fácil quitar la capa exterior de piel. Lavalos,quitando la capa externa, estarán suaves y podras quitarles las venas también.

Parte los chiles ya desvenados en tiras

En una olla (de preferencia de barro) pon a acitronar media cebolla en rodajas finas. Cuando la cebolla este doradita (color trigo), agrega las rajas de poblano Una vez que esten doradas de forma uniforme,agrega 1 litro de crema. Se sazona con Knorr suiza como sustituto de sal.

CERDO EN VERDOLAGAS

500 g de pulpa de cerdo en trozos
8 tomates verdes medianos
5 chiles serranos
Media cebolla
4 dientes de ajo
1 manojo de cilantro
1 cucharada de comino
200 grs de verdolagas (limpias y desinfectadas)
Pimienta al gusto
Tempo de preparación: 20 min

La pulpa de cerdo se pone a cocer unos 20 min. Se pasa un sarten para dorarla un poco con aceite Salsa:

Se ponen a cocer los tomates verdes y los chiles. Una vez listos, se vacian en la licuadora con una tercera parte del agua en la cual los cociste. Se agrega la cebolla, cilantro (crudos) y la cucharada de comino

En un sarten, se pone la salsa, se agrega la carne y las verdolagas, Sal y pimienta al gusto.

PASTA LINGUINI A LA NARANJA

1 paquete de 200-300 grs de linguini
1/2 lt. De crema acida
1 raza de jugo de naranja 1 chorrito de vino blanco
1/2 cebolla
1 ramito de perejil
3 chiles serranos
250 gramos de camarones pacotilla precocidos
Tiempo de preparación: 20 min.

La pasta se pone a cocer en agua, una ves que esta al dente, reserva
En una cazuela, pon a dorar la cebolla, el chile y el perejil, finamente picados . Agrega el vino, jugo de naranja y la crema. Por aparte, pon adorar ligeramente los camarones con un poco de mantequilla . Incorpora la pasta y los camarones. No calentar por mucho tiempo para evitar que los camarones se sequen y se pongan duros . Puedess decorar con una ramita de perejil al centro al emplatar.

Recipe and scripture by: Sandy Hudson (San Miguel Allende)

1 Corinthians 13:13 and now these three things remain: faith , hope and love. But the greatest of these is love.

RACHEL'S FABULOUS SQUASH RECIPE

3 lb squash – sliced, cooked, well drained and mashed
5 T butter – divided
1 / 2 cup chopped onion
1 cup cheddar cheese – shredded
2 large eggs – beaten
1/ 4 mayo
2 t sugar
1 t salt
20 Ritz or saltine crackers – crushed

Melt 4 t butter, saute onion. Remove from heat. Stir in squash into a greased 11 X 7 baking dish. Melt remaining 1 t butter crackers. Bake 350 for 30 minutes. This does a half recipe. Enjoy!

Receta y escritura de: Claudia Cantu de Fuentes (San Miguel Allende)

Proverbios 16:3 Encomienda a Jehova tus obras, y tus pensamientos serán afirmados.

ARROZ VERDE
Ingredientes

1 tz de Arroz
Aceite
1 diente de ajo
1 trozo de cebolla cruda
1/4 manojo de cilantro
1/4 de pimiento verde
Sal mar y pimienta al gusto

Preparacion:

Colocan los siguientes ingredientes en crudo en la licuadora
Pimiento verde, cilantro, cebolla y ajo. Sal y pimienta y un poco de comino en polvo y 2 tazas de agua. En una cacerola se fríe con aceite el arroz hasta que quede color dorado, después anadimos la mezcla de la licuadora, se menea y se tapa hasta que quede listo.
Nota: El arroz se puede cocer en agua, solo que se cocer en agua, con la mezcla que se preparo en la licuadora.

Recipe and scripture by: " Translated from Russian by Olga Kolesnikova Ph.D. in Computer Science (Mexico city)

Colossians: 3:23 Whatever you do, work at it with all your heart, as working for the Lord, not for men.

RUSSIAN SALAD

Ingredients:

Sausage 200 g
Salted cucumbers or pickles 100 g
Canned green peas 350 g
Mayonnaise 50 g
Potatoes 300 g
Eggs 4
Carrots 100 g
Salt

Preparation:
Boil potatoes and carrots in advance. If you cook vegetables in one pot, you have to take into account that potatoes cook a Little faster tan carrots. Therefore, the potatoes must be removed from the boiling water a little a earlier. Cool and peel boiled vegetables. Also boil the required amount of eggs. Then prepare the rest of the ingredients. Cut the boiled sausage and pickles into small cubes. Cut boiled potatoes and carrots into the same size. Chop boiled eggs finely with a knife or grate them on a coarse grater. During the cutting process, all the ingredients can be immediately transferred to one large salad bowl, at the end add canned peas and salt to your taste. Before serving the salad, season with mayonnaise and canned green peas.

Recipe and scripture by: Donna Tanner (San Miguel Allende)

Psalm 37: 3-4

"Trust in the Lord and do good; dwell in the land and enjoy safe pasture. Delight yourself in the Lord and he will give you the desires of your heart."

BROCCOLI PIE

2 package chopped frozen broccoli
12 eggs
2 oz. Softened cream cheese
4 handfuls bean sprouts
4 ladies handfuls shredded sharp cheddar
8 chopped green onions
4 heaping tablespoons parmesan cheese
Salt and pepper to taste (shake , shake, shake)

Cook and drain broccoli (in microwave. So it is hot when mixed). Beat eggs. Add cheese and stir in remaining ingredients. Bake at 425 degrees for 45 minutes, until golden brown around edges: Cool 10 minutes.

Substitute w/spinach and red onions instead of broccoli

Clementina London Nigerian (Mexico City)

Nigerian Soup

This recipe will show you how to make this popular West African soup with melon seeds.

1 cup blended onion (about 3-5 and fresh chilies, to taste)
1 cups egusi (melon seeds, ground or milled)
1/2 – cup palm oil
1 teaspoons fresh Une (Iru, locust beans)
Salt (to taste)
Ground crayfish (to taste)
7-8 cups stock
Cooked meat and fish (quantity and variety to personal preference)
1 cups cut pumpkin leaves
1 cup waterleaf (cut)
3 tablespoons bitter leaf (washed)

EGUSI PASTE: Prepare the egusi paste:
Blend egusi seeds and onion mixture. Set aside. MAKE

THE Soup:

In a large pot, heat the palm oil on medium for a minute and then add the Une.

Slowly add the stock and set on low heat to simmer. Scoop teaspoon size balls of the egusi paste

mixture into the stock. Be sure to keep ball shape.

Leave to simmer for 20-30 min. so the balls cook through. Add the meat and fish and other bits which you´d like to use. Add cut -up pumpkin leaves. Add the waterleaf. Stir and put a lid on the pot and allow cook for 7-10 min. Till the leaves wilt. Add the bitter leaf. Leave the lid off while the cooking finishes for another 5-10 min. Stir check seasoning and adjust accordingly.

Now you can sit back and enjoy your Delicious Nigerian Egusi Soup

Recipe by: Clementina London Nigerian (Mexico City)

WHITE RICE AND EFO RIRO
Ingredients

200 g African spinach
100 g bell pepper
200 g tomatoes
1 knorr cube To taste
Salt
100 g palm oil
200 g pomo (cow skin)
1 onion medium sized STEPS

Wash and cut pomo into bits and boil for 10 min. Cut vegetables and wash

Blend tomatoes and pepper and an onion with little water
Pour palm oil and when hot add your blended mix with the boiled pomo for 5-10 min.

Add the vegetables and salt and Knorr cube for 5 min.

Food is ready to serve

Recipe and scripture by: Clementina London (Mexico City)

Zechariah 8:12 For there will be peace for the seed: the vine will yield its fruit, the land will yield its produce and the heavens will give their dew; and I will cause the remnant of this people to inherit all these things.

CHICKEN JOLLOF RICE RECIPE BY TASTY

Ingredients For 6 servings

6 medium tomatoes, sliced
2 red bell pepper, stemmed, seeded and quartered
2 small red onions, 1 quartered, 1 diced
1 scotch Bonnet pepper, or habanero, stem removed
1/2 cup vegetable oil (120 mL) plus 2 tablespoons
2 lb boneless chicken thighs (450 g) cubed
2 teaspoons curry powder
2 teaspoon dried thyme
3 cups parboiled long grain rice (400 g) washed
 STOCK
stock cubes and 3/4 cup water

Preparation

Add the tomatoes, red bell pepper, quartered onion, and pepper to a blender and blend until smooth. In a poto ver medium heat, add 2 tablespoons oil, diced red onion, chicken, and curry poweder. Cook until onions are soft and chicken has browned form pot and set aside.

Raise heat to medium-high, and using the same pot, add pureed tomato mixture, cooking until reduced by half.

Add in remaining oil, and fry sauce for 8-10 min.

Stir in chicken, along with rice, stock and thyme leaves.

Cover pot tightly with foil. Cover with lid and reduce heat to low, cooking for 30 min. Once rice is cooked, fluff up before serving.

Enjoy

Recipe and scriptures: Janice Driscoll (San Miguel Allende)

Isaiah 53: 4,5 Surely he took up our infirmities and carried our sorrows, yet we considered him stricken by God, smitten by him, and afflicted. But he was pierced for our transgressions, he was crushed for our iniquities; the punishment that brought us peace was upon him, and by his wounds we are healed.
Isaiah 26: 3,4 You will keep in perfect peace him whose mind is steadfast, because he trust in you. Trust in the Lord forever, for the Lord, is the Rock eternal.

BROCCOLI SALAD
Ingredients

Half a pound of bacon chopped
One large broccoli
2 cups of chopped celery
6 small green onions
One cup of chopped pecans
One cup of cran-raisins
2 cups of seedless grapes
Dressing
One cup of mayonnaise
1/4 cup of milk
1 tbsp of vinegar
Quarter cup of sugar (pr as desired)

Stir together the mayonnaise, the milk, vinegar and the sugar and then stir into the broccoli and the rest of the ingredients.

Recipe and scritpure by: Ruth Johnston (Mexico City)

Matthew 13: 31-32 He told them another parable: " The kingdom of heaven is like a mustard seed, which a man took and planted in his field. Though it is the smallest of all your seeds, yet when it grows, it is the largest of garden plants and becomes a tree, so that the birds of the air come and perch in its branches."

TRADITIONAL IRISH COLCANNON RECIPE

Creamy mashed potatoes, kale, and onion are mixed together to create this wonderful traditional.

Ingredients:

22 ounces floury potatoes (baking potatoes, peeled and quartered)
4 ounces curly kale
 (or spring cabbage, chopped)
1/2 cup spring onions (roughly chopped)
1/4 cup spring onions (finely choped)
4 ounces butter

Recipe by: Pam Breyer   (San Miguel Allende)

Matthew 4:4 Man does not live on bread alone, but on every word that comes from the mouth of God.
CREAM CORN

Ingredients:

2 tablespoon butter
2 tablespoon flour
1 1/2 cup half and half (half milk and half cream)
2 teaspoon chicken bouillon 2 tablespoon sugar
2 packages corn thawed

Preparation:

Mix butter and flour (thicken)
Mix all ingredients   Pour the corn (Do not cook the corn, only heat it)
Put it in a casserole and warm it in the oven

Recta de Maria Del Socorro Maldonado Hdez. Casa ABIERTA AL Tiempo 5483-4000 ext. 1772 (Cuidad de Mexico)

PASTEL DE CHOCOLATE

Ingredientes:

2 tazas de harina de trigo, taza y media de azúcar, una y media mantequilla Gloria de 90 gms.3/4 de taza de coco Hersey, 4 huevos a temperatura ambiente, 3/4 de taza de leche, 2 cucharaditas de royal, una cucharadita de extracto de vainilla y una pizca de sal.

Preparacion:

Se ciema la harina, la cocoa, el royal y la pizca de sal y todo eso se incorpora bien, se deja por separado.

Se derrite la mantequilla en el bol de cristal 40 segundos en el horno de microondas y se le incorporal la leche, huevos, azúcar y la vainilla. Se mezcla todo con la batidora por espacio de 3 a 4 minutos, se va incorporando la harina de poco en poco con los ingredientes ya integrados (cocoa, royal, sal) a que se incorporen muy bien y se sigue batiendo hasta considerar que ya esta listo para vaciando al monde previamente engrasado.

El horno ya debe de estar caliente a temperatura 200 grados. Se mete el molde y se baja la temperatura a 160 grados por espacio de 40 minutos o considerar que ya esta listo.

Se puede bañar con chocolate amargo derretido en baño maría.

Recipe and scripture by: Sandra Orellana Writer (San Miguel Allende)

Psalm 107: 9 For he satisfies the thirsty and fills the hungry with good things.

BROCCOLI CASSEROLE
Ingredients:

2 pkg. Frozen chopped broccoli cooked 1 can mushroom soup
1 small jar cheese–whiz Cracker crumbs (Ritz) Instructions:
Cook broccoli, saute add all ingredients. Top with cracker crumbs and bake at 350 for 30-40 min.

Recipe and scripture: Vanessa D'Rand (mother's recipe) (San Miguel Allende)

Romans 8:28 And we know that all things work together for good to them that love God, to them who are called according to his purpose.

CHICKEN A L'ORANGE

Ingredients:

3 chicken breasts, cut in half
1/2 cup butter
1/4 cup flour
2 T. brown sugar
1 t. salt r
1/2 cup orange juice
1/2 cup water

Brown chicken slowly in butter. Remove from pan. Blend flour, sugar, salt, pepper, and ginger into drippings in pan. Cook on low for one minute, stirring constantly. Stir in Orange juice and water slowly until it thickens and boils one minute. Return chicken to pan. Simmer covered until chicken reaches 165 degrees in the center, approximately 30-40 min.

Notes:

Kathleen O´Grady y Family Recipes

I love to cook. The planning, chopping, sautéing, baking , smells, tastes. I go into my own, relaxing zone without realizing how many hours have passed. Every day it's like a special little gift . I can give to my family and friends. Years ago when I was recently married, my mother gave me a tin with a " special " ingredient to add to a lot of my dishes to make them delicious. Inside was a recipe card in her written, " Prepare everything with love" That was over 33 years ago when I first arrived in San Miguel de Allende. There were no big supermarkets or specialty shops and a lot of the ingredients I was used to cooking with I couldn't find. So I would come up with substitutions. And baking at high altitudes was another matter. My first Christmas here all of my mother's and grandmother's cookie recipes melted into one, flat cookie in the oven. I eventually figured out the adjustments through trial and error. Slowly I got used to the beautiful, colorful fresh markets and began to learn how to prepare Mexican dishes, especially from my sweet, Oaxacan mother in law, Guadalupe. As a result my children have grown up with a menagerie of recipes from my family, my husband's family and recipes from all over the world. As Julia Child said, " Try new recipes, learn from your mistakes, be fearless, and above all, have fun! "

Kathleen O´Grady

Recipe: Kathy O'Grady (San Miguel Allende)

Psalm 16:6 "The lines have fallen to me in pleasant places, indeed, my heritage is beautiful to me."

Swedish cookie from my great great grandmother Ann Sandburg was born in Aneby, Smaland Sweden in 1861 and moved to the USA in the early 1880's In the picture she is holding my mother Sharon about 1942.

SNOBOLLAR COOKIES

Ingredients:

1 cup unsalted butter, softened 4 tablespoons powdered sugar
1 teaspoon salt
1 table spoon vanilla extra
2 cups flour, sifted
2 cups pecans finely ground
Powdered sugar for dusting About 1-2 cups

Preheat oven to 325 F Grease the cookie sheets with butter. Have a bowl with about 1 cup of powdered sugar ready. In another bowl , cream the butter . Mix in the powdered sugar and salt. Then add the vanilla and mix. Add the flour and pecans and mix well. Roll into small balls and place, on cookie sheets about 1 ½ inches apart Bake in oven 18-30 min. Watch carefully starting at 18 min. So they don't brown. Remove from oven and while still warm roll in the powdered sugar and place on a cooling rack.

When they're cool, roll them again in the powdered sugar, adding more powdered sugar to the bowl as needed.

Recipe and scripture by: Kathy O'Grady (San Miguel Allende)

Recipe from Kathy's great grandmother Nell Sandburg weeks. She´s the daughter of of Anna Sandbourg and lived most of her life in Corralitos, California.

Proverbs 16:24 "Gracious words are a honeycomb, sweet to the soul and healing to the bones."

NANA NELL'S APPLE PUDDING CAKE

Ingredients:

1 cup sugar
1/4 cup soft butter
1 egg, beaten
2 cups unpeeled shredded apples
1 cup flour, sifted 1 teaspoon baking soda 1 teaspoon baking soda
1 teaspoon cinnamon 3/4 teaspoon nutmeg 1/4 teaspoon salt
1/4 cup chopped walnuts

Preheat oven to 350 F Grease an 8 inch square baking dish. In a large bowl cream the butter and sugar together until well mixed and fluffy. Add egg and apples. Mix well. Add the rest of the dry ingredients and mix. Pour into the greased dish. Bake for about 45 min.

Serve as is or with:

1 cup heavy whipping cream whipped with 2 tablespoons of honey and 2 tablespoons of whiskey. Or with: Lemon sauce

1/2 cup sugar
1 tablespoon cornstarch
1/4 cup cold water
1/2 cup boiling water
1 tablespoons butter
2 tablespoons lemon juice

Mix sugar and cornstarch together in a small saucepan. Mix in cold water until dissolved. Add boiling water and cook over medium heat stirring constantly until thickened. Remove from heat and stir in butter and lemon juice.

Recipe and scripture by Kathy O'Grady (San Miguel Allende)

Matthew 6:11 "Give us this day our daily bread."

Recipe from my grandpa Harold Weeks Zook. He was a purple heart recipient from WWII. He loved to cook. Heps Nell Sandburg Weeks son. This recipe is a favorite in our family.

SHERRIED ARTICHOKE CHICKEN

Ezekiel 24:4 "Put into it the pieces of meat, all the choice pieces- the leg and the shoulder. Fill it with the best of these bones."

Ingredients:

1 frying chicken, about 3 ½ lbs cut in pieces
Salt, pepper and paprika
6 tablespoons butter
1 (1 lb) can artichoke hearts, drained
1/4 lb fresh mushrooms, thinly sliced
3 tables minced onion
2 tablespoons flour
2/3 cup chicken broth
1/4 cup sherry
1 teaspoon Rosemary

Sprinkle chicken generously with salt, pepper and paprika. Ina large, heavy skillet, brown chicken pieces on all sides in 4 tablespoon of the butter. Transfer to a 2 quart casserole dish. Arrange artichoke hearts between the chicken pieces . Add remaining 2 tablespoons of butter to the drippings in the skillet and melt. Add the mushrooms and onion sautéing until tender. Sprinkle flour over mushrooms and cook for a few seconds. Stir in chicken broth, sherry and Rosemary. Cook stirring constantly for a few min. Until thickened . Pour over chicken. Cover and bake in a 375 F oven for about 40 min. Serve with rice spooning some of the sauce over it.

Recipe and scripture by: Kath O'Grady

Recipe from my mother, Sharon Zook O'Grady. She is Harold Zook's daughter. She liked to cook Irish food for my dad, Patrick O'Grady especially o St. Patrick's Day. She may have gotten this recipe from his side of the family.

IRISH SODA BREAD

Ingredients:

4 cups flour
1 teaspoon baking soda
1 teaspoon cream of tartar 1 teaspoon salt
3/4 cup sugar
1/2 cup butter, melted 1/3 cup raisins
2 teaspoon caraway seeds 1 3/4 cups buttermilk

Preheat oven to 375 F Butter and flour a large baking sheet. Sift the dry ingredients into a large bowl. Mix in the raisins and caraway seeds. Add the butter and buttermilk. Mix well making a soft, moist dough. Add more flour Little by Little if dough is too sticky to handle. Transfer dough to a lightly floured Surface and knead for 3-4 min. Until dough is firm. Shape into two, round loaves. Place onto prepared baking sheet. Score each loaf with an "X" on top. Brush with buttermilk and dust with flour. Bake until nicely browned for about 1 hour. Cool on a wire rack.

Recipe and scripture by: Kathy O´Grady (San Miguel Allende)

Genesis 9:3 "Everything that lives and moves will be food for you. Just as I gave you the green plants, I now give you everything."

This recipe goes back to my great-grandmother Katie Flanagan O´Grady. Her family was from Borris-in-Ossory, Laois Country, Ireland. She was born in Iowa in 1865. This recipe is traditionally served in the fall around All Hallow´s Eve as a main dish.

Colcannon (cal ceann fhionn)

Ingredients:

1 lb cabbage, cored, shredded and chopped
2 lbs potatoes peeled and quartered
1 large leek washed and sliced white part only
1 cup mild Salt and pepper
½ teaspoon mace
1 stick of butter
Heavy cream

Boil potatoes in a pot of salted water until soft. Drain . Boil the cabbage in another pot of salted water until tender. Drain. In another large pot cook leeks in mild over medium heat for about 10 min. Add the cooked potatoes and cabbage. Mash all together and add mace and salt and pepper to taste. Add the butter and some cream. Mash until creamy and dot with about 2 tablespoons more of butter.

Bain taitneamh as do bheile!

Receta y escritura de: Kathy O'Grady (San Miguel Allende)

Ezekial 24:10 "So heap on the wood and Kindle the fire. Cook the meat well, mixing in the **spices***; and let the bones be charred."*

This is a very typical German meat recipe from my dad´s mom´s side of the family. His mother was Ruth Hertha Frieda Haas is my "Gram" She understood some German and always said to me "Ich liebe dich".

SAUERBRATEN

Ingredients:

4 lb piece of beef rump, Chuck or round roast
Salt and pepper
1 cup red wine vinegar
1 cup red wine
3 cups water
2 yellow onions, sliced
4 bay leaves
12 peppercorns
4 whole cloves
2 sliced carrots
2-3 tablespoons of bacon oil for browning
1/3 cup flour
1/4 cup sugar white or brown
2-3 gingersnap cookies, crushed

Sprinkle meat with salt and pepper. In a big glass bowl mix together the vinegar, wine, water, onions, carrots and spices. Add the meat and cover tightly. Put it in the refrigerator for at least 4-5 days and every day turn the meat once or twice. Remove meat and wipe dry. Strain the vegetables from the wine marinade and set both aside. Grease a heavy roasting pan with bacon Grease or oil and sear meat on all sides. Add the strained vegetables and cook for 5 min. Add the wine marinade. Roast in 300 F oven for 2 hours , basting meat every once in awhile. When the meat is almost done sprinkle sugar over meat.

Roast 5-10 min. Turning meat until sugar dissolves. Mix flour with some water and add to marinade along with the gingersnaps. Pour over meat and roast 1/2 hour or more until gravy is thick and meat is tender. Strain the gravy. Add more salt and pepper if needed. Slice the meat and serve with gravy, boiled potatoes or potato pancakes and rotkraut (a red cabbage dish) Mahlzeit!

Recipe and scripture by: Kathy O´Grady

2 Thessalonians 3:10 "For even when we were with you , we would give you this command: If anyone is not willing to work, let him note at."

This recipe is from my mom´s maternal side of the family. They were old California hispanic families that came over from Spain. This is an enchilada recipe from my nana Rachel Castro and her mom Frances Litllejohn Castro. I´ve had to change it a Little bit because I can´t get the same dried chiles (Anaheim and New Mexican) that they use in California. So I substituted with guajillo and ancho chiles. A little bit spicier, but not much.

CALIFORNIA ENCHILADAS

For enchilada sauce
1 dried guajillo chiles, stems and seeds removed
2 dried ancho chiles, stems and seeds removed
1 tablespoon apple vinegar
1 cup chicken broth
2 cups water, more or less
4 tomatoes, stewed in water just enough to remove skins
1/4 cup olive oil
1 onion, chopped
3 garlic cloves, minced
1 1/2 teaspoons cumin
2 teaspoons oregano
1/ 2 teaspoon salt

Fill a small pot with a few cups of water, vinegar and the chiles. Bring to a boil. Turn off, cover and let sit for 15-20 min. Drain chiles reserving 1 cup of the liquid. In a large frying pan heat the olive oil and saute the onions and garlic for about 8 min.

In a blender add the chiles, 1 cup of the reserved chile liquid, 1 cup chicken broth, the prepared tomatoes, the onion and garlic, cumin, oregano and salt. Blend well. Add back to the large frying pan and add Little by Little the 2 cups water until it has the right consistency. Simmer gently for about 15 min. stirring often. Adjust seasonings.

For filling:
Tortillas flour or corn, around 12 or more 3 lbs yellow onions, chopped
1/4 cup olive oil
1/2 lb cheddar cheese, grated
1/2 lb Monterey Jack cheese, grated
2 cans black, California olives,chopped

In a large frying pan saute the onions in oil and a little bit of water on low heat, stirring often for about 20 min.
To assemble, heat oven to 350 F. Spread some of the enchilada sauce in the bottom of a 9x13 inch baking dish. Dip tortillas in hot vegetable oil in a small frying pan. Pat off extra oil. Dip the tortilla one at a time in the enchilada sauce, Place it on a plate and fill with cooked onions, about ¼ cup of the cheeses and 1 tablespoon of black olives. Roll up tightly and place into the baking dish. Repeat with the rest of the tortillas until onions are used up. Generously pour enchilada sauce on top and sprinkle with remaining cheese and olives. Bake until heated through and cheese is melted about 40 min. If there is any extra enchilada sauce, it can be frozen for later use.

Provecho!

This is a recipe from Salomon Maawad's mom, Guadalup Velasuez Ramirez. Salomon Maawad Velasquez : Jazz musician and composer. The Downbeats Jazz Quarter available for private events. Contractor for house building and remodeling. Real Estate Agent
Celular # 4151030236

"Doña Lupita." She was from San Miguel Peras, Oaxaca up in the sierra. She also loved to cook and had such a good "sazon." She never measured anything. It was always a handfull of this or a pinch of that.

She taught me quite a few oaxacan dishes. I´d always grab her hand and try to measure out what she was putting in the pot and she'd just laugh. She was the sweetest person ever.

Song of Songs 5:16 "Eat, friends, and drink; drink your fill of love."

CHILES PASILLA RELLENOS DE OAXACA DE DOÑA LUPITA

Ingredientes:

25 chiles pasilla de Oaxaca
1 chuchara de vinagre de manazana
4 muslos y 1 pechuga de pollo
Cebolla y ajo
1 raja pequeña de canela
8-10 clavos enteros
1 cebolla blanca chica, picada
3 dientes de ajo, picado
3/4 - 1 kilo de jitomate, picado Un puño de perejil, picado
50 gramos de almendra sin cascara, picada
50 gramos de pasas
1 cucharadita de azúcar 1 cucharadita de vinagre
1 cubo de Knorr pollo
huevos, separados
Harina
Aceite

Remoja los chiles pasilla en agua caliente con el vinagre durante una hora para suavizarlos. Pon el pollo a cocinar en agua con cebolla, ajo y sal unos 45 min. Una vez que este cocido, hay que desmenuzarlo. En un molcajete chico, muele la canela y los clavos finamente. En una olla grande sofríe en aceite caliente la cebolla primero, luego el ajo, y luego el jitomate.

Agrega el perejil, la canela y clavos, las almendras, las pasas, azúcar, vinagre y Knorr pollo. Agrega el pollo desmenuzado. Cocina por unos 30 min. Deja enfriar. Saca los chiles pasilla del agua y los corta de un lado para sacar las semillas y venas. Secalos con una toalla y rellenalos con el guisado de pollo.

Para capear los chiles, pasalos en harina y reserva todos en un plato. En un tazon para mezclar, bate las claras hasta que están rigidas y agrega las yemas una por una. En un sarten con aceite caliente, deja caer un poco del huevo batido. Con mucho cuidado, coloca uno de los chiles rellenos en el centro de la mezcla de huevo y envuelve con mucho cuidado. Cuando esta dorado de los dos lados, pon el chile en un plato que tiene Servitoalla. Repite con todos los chiles. Sirvelos acompañados con frijoles negros de la olla, arroz blanco, totillas de puro maíz y una copita de mezcal. Buen provecho!

Recipe and scriptures by Salomon's father, Don Rodrigo Salomon Maawad Salibet, showed his wife, Doña, as to how he wanted his lebanese food prepared. Of course she would sometimes slip in a bit of serrano chiles just to spice things up. And then she went on to teach me so I could make them for Salomon. Sadly he never really knew his father because he died suddenly when he was 1 year old. But maybe in a way he knew something about his father through these dishes.

Ecclesiastes 9:7 "Go, eat your food with gladness, and drink your wine with a joyful heart, for it is now that God favors what you do."

KIBBEH CHAROLA (kibbeh bil-Sanieh)

Para el relleno:

6 cucharas de mantequilla 1/3 taza de piñones
1 cebolla grande picada finamente
200 gms de carne molida (res o carnero) cucharaditas de canela molida
2 cucharaditas de pimienta gorda molida 1 pizca de nuez moscada
1/2 cucharadita de pimienta negra Sal a gusto

Derrite la mantequilla en un sarten y frie los piñones hasta que queden un poco dorados. Retiralos a un plato. En la misma mantequilla frie la cebolla hasta que quede suave. Agrega la carne y frie hasta que queda bien cocia y en pedazos chicos. Quita el sarten de la flama y agrega las especies y los piñones.

Para el Kibbeh:

1 cebolla cortada en pedazos
500 grms de carnero (pierna) o res (aguayón) sin hueso, piel, grasa y molido
1/4 kilo de trigo árabe (bulgur)
Un puño de hierbabuena picada
1/2 cucharadita comino molido Sal y pimienta
1 chile verde sin semillas y venas, picado (opcional)
6 cucharas de mantequilla derretida o aceite de oliva

Pre calienta el horno a 200 C. En un cuenco pon el trigo árabe y enjuague 2 o 3 veces. Agrega sufficiente agua para tapar el trigo y dejalo remojando durante 15 min. Una vez listo, exprimelo bien. En un procesador, pon los pedazos de cebolla y procesa hasta que quede finamente picada.

Agrega la carne, hierbabuena, sal, pimienta, comino,(Chile) y el trigo árabe bien exprimido Muele todo muy bien. Engrasa un recipiente de horno rectangular con mantequilla. Coloca la mitad de la mezcla de carne con bulgur en el recipiente y cubre el fondo con u na capa lisa usando tus manos huedas para

apretarla. Toma el resto de la carne y extiende sobre el relleno con otra capa lisa con tus manos húmedas y aprieta bien. Marcar ligeramente con un cuchillo unos patrones geométricos de tu propia creación.

Vierte la mantequilla derretida o el aciete de oliva encima y extiende bien.Tapa el recipiente con aluminio y hornea por 40-50 ,om. Quita el aluminio y hornea por 10 -15 min. Mas o hasta que la carne se dore.

Se puede servir caliente o a temperatura con jocoque o hummus, una ensalada de jitomate, pepino y cebolla cambray y una copa de vino. Bel hana wel she fa!

Hummus be-Tah ineh

1 lata de garbanzos cocidos
1/3 taza de liquido de los garbanzos
1/3 taza jugo de limon
2-3 ajos
1 taza de tahini Sal
Pimenton Aceite de oliva

En un procesador agrega los garbanzos, el liquido de garbanzos, y ajos. Procesa bien. Agrega el tahini y el jugo de limon poco a poco a su gusto. Si el pure es muy espeso, agrega un poco de agua hasta que queda suave y cremoso. Pruebalo y agrega sal a su gusto . Para servir, ponlo en un tazon. Haz un hoyo en medio y agrega al hoyo 2 cucharas de aceite de olviva. En las orillas rocia el pimenton. Sirve con pan de pita.

Ensalada de jitomate, pepino y cebolla cambray pepinos pelados y rebanados
8 jitomates rebanados
2-3 cebollas cambray, rebanadas 1-2 ajos, pelados y machucados
Jugo de 1 limon amarillo, o menos a su gusto
4 cucharas de aceite de oliva
15 hojas de hierbabuena Sal y pimienta

En un molcajete chico muele el ajo con una pizca de sal y la hierbabuena hasta que forme una pasta. Agrega el jugo de lion y luego el aciete de oliva. Sal y pimienta a su gusto. Rocialo arriba de la verdura.

Maawad Family Recipes 138

Notes:

Notes:

Desserts

Recipe by Lynn Ramsey St. Paul's Church Despensa Project (San Miguel de Allende)

LEMON THUMBPRINT COOKIES

A recipe from a dear friend's sweet departed mother

¾ cup very finely chopped pecans. Save to roll cookies in. Mix
¼ cup soft shortening
¼ cup soft butter
¼ cup brown sugar Packed
1 egg yolk. Save the egg white for rolling cookies in
½ teaspoon vanilla
Sift together 1 cup sifted flour
¼ teaspoon salt

Add to the butter, brown sugar, yolk and vanilla.

Mix. Roll into small balls the size of walnuts.

Beat the egg white slightly with a fork, you can add few drops of water to the egg white then thin it. Roll cookie dough ball in the egg yolks and then in the finely chopped pecans.

Place 1 inch apart on a parchment lined cookie sheet and bake 350 degrees for 5 minutes.

Remove from oven and press your thumb or finger in the center of the cookie, do not press all the way through. Bake another 8 minutes. Cool

Filling:

8 oz cream cheese

1 box powder sugar sifted 1 teaspoon vanilla

You may need to add a few drops of milk to get the right consistency Mix and then fill the thumb print with icing filling

Recipe and scripture by Marsha Velazquez St. Paul's Church   (San Miguel de Allende)

Hebrews 13:5 "Let your character be free from the love of money and be satisfied with what you have, for God, Himself he said, I will not in any way fail. You nor give you up, nor leave you without support. I will not leave you helpless nor forsake you or let you down! Assuredly not!"

BERRY-CHIA CRUMBLE

This is a low sugar, high protein dessert.

Ingredients:

6 cups of frozen berries
¼ cup of chia
¼ cup of pure honey
2 cups of almond flour
¼ cup of coconut oil
1 teaspoon vanilla extract
1 cup of chopped pecans or almonds

Instructions:

Preheat oven to 350 Defrost berries and drain of the juice and save it.
Grease a 9x13 inch glass baking dish with coconut oil.

Pour the berries and chia into the baking dish.
Combine honey, berry juice and vanilla.

Blend flour, coconut oil and chopped nuts until crumbly texture. Spread it evenly in the berries and chia mixture then spread evenly the crumbly flour, oil and nuts mixture.

Bake for 30 to 35 minutes, until the top is golden brown and the edges are bubbling.

Recipe and scripture by Marsha Velazquez St. Paul's Church (San Miguel de Allende)

Nehemiah 8:10 " Be not grieved and depressed, for the Lord is your strength and your stronghold. "

APPLE CUSTARD

This is a low sugar dessert, but very tasty.

Ingredients:

4 large eggs
½ cup of sugar
½ cup flour
1 ¼ cups skim milk
1 teaspoon vanilla extract
1 apple peeled
½ cup raisins
1 tablespoon butter

Instructions:

Preheat oven to 400 F and grease a 9 inch pie plate with butter. Mix well eggs and sugar. Whisk in flour, milk and vanilla.

Cut apple into thin slices and place in concentric circles on the bottom of the pie plate. Gently pour the egg/milk/flour mixture over the apple slices.

Put tiny pats of butter on top and then sprinkle 2 tablespoons of sugar mixed with cinnamon on top. Place the pie plate on top of a baking sheet and bake for 25 to 30 minutes.

Let cool and then serve.

Recipe and scripture by Jenny Kersten St. Paul's Church (San Miguel de Allende)

1 Corinthians 10:13 No temptation has seized you except what is common to man. And God is faithful;he will not let you be tempted beyond what you can bear. But when you are tempted, he will also provide a way out so that you can stand up under it.

CATNIP COOKIES

Ingredients:

1 cup whole wheat flour
¼ cup soy flour 1 teaspoon catnip
1 egg
1/3 cup milk
2 tablespoons wheat germ
1/3 cup powdered milk
1 tablespoon unsulfured molasses
2 tablespoons unsalted butter or vegetable oil

Instructions:

Preheat oven to 350 degrees F.

Mix dry ingredients together, then add molasses, egg, oil and milk.

Roll out dough flat onto a greased cookie sheet and cut into small pieces.
Bake for 20 minutes.

Store in sealed container.

Hymn Quote

"All things bright and beautiful, all creatures great and small, all things wise and wonderful, The Lord God made them all."

Recipe and scripture by Jenny Ann Kersten St. Paul's Church (San Miguel de Allende)

1 Corinthians 10:13: No temptation has seized you except what is common to men. And God is faithful; he will not let let you be tempted beyond what you can bear. But when you are tempted, he will also provide a way out so that you can stand up under it.

APPLE CRANBERRY CAKE

Ingredients:

½ pound unsalted butter
½ teaspoon salt
2 eggs
1 cup sugar
2 cups flour
1 teaspoon baking powder
1 teaspoon baking soda
1 teaspoon ground cinnamon
1 cup chopped apples
1 cup whole fresh or frozen cranberries
½ cup seeds or nuts

Instructions:

Cream butter.

Mix in salt, eggs and sugar.

Add the flour sifted with the baking soda, baking powder and cinnamon and mix well. Add the fruit and the seeds or nuts.

Bake in an 8x8 inch pan or an 8 inch cake pan.

Bake in a 350 degree oven for 40 to 45 minutes or until a cake tester or toothpick comes out clean.

Recipe and scripture by Jenny Ann Kersten St. Paul's Church (San Miguel de Allende)

1 Corinthians 10:13: No temptation has seized you except what is common to men. And God is faithful; he will not let let you be tempted beyond what you can bear. But when you are tempted, he will also provide a way out so that you can stand up under it.

SCOTTISH SHORTBREAD

Ingredients:

1 pound butter, softened
1 cup sugar
1/2 tsp salt
4-6 cups sifted all purpose flour, plus more for dusting

Instructions:

Preheat the oven to 350 degrees F

Begin by creaming the butter and sugar in a large mixing bowl.

Add the salt to the first cup of flour and mix with the butter mixture by stirring in using a wooden spoon. Add the flour slowly until the mixture can be worked by hand, then place the mixture on a board or counter that has been lightly dusted with flour to avoid sticking.

Dust your hands with flour, then work the flour into butter mixture until it begins to crumble and not hold together.

Now, place the mixture on a heavy Steel baking pan or cookie sheet, and spread out to cover the pan entirely.

Prick all over with a fork.

Bake until golden brown, about 25 minutes. Let cool. Cut immediately.

Recipe by Jenny Kersten St. Paul's Church (San Miguel de Allende)

PEANUT BUTTER CUPCAKES

Ingredients:

1 /1/4 Cups all purpose flour
1 cup firmly packed light brown sugar
¾ cup milk
¼ cup peanut butter
1 egg
1 tablespoon buttr or margarine, softened
1 tablespoon vegetable oil
1 teaspoon vanilla extract
1 ½ teaspoon baking powder
½ teaspoon salt
½ cup semisweet chocolate chips
Peanut butter frosting (recipe follows)
2/3 cup chopped honey-roasted peanuts (optional)

Instructions:

Preheat Oven to 350 F (175 C)

Combine all ingredients except frosting and peanuts in blend.

Cover and blend at high speed about 45 seconds, stopping motor once or twice to scrape down sides. Pour into muffin tins fitted with paper cupcake liners, filling each about 2/3 full.

Bake 25 to 30 minutes, until toothpick inserted in center comes out clean.
Cool cupcakes completely.

Spread with frosting. If desired, garnish with chopped honey-roasted peanuts.

Devil's Food Fudge

Frosting 3 cups powdered sugar
½ cup unsweetened cocoas powder
½ cup (1 stick) butter or margarine, softened 3 tablespoons water or cold, strong coffee
1 teaspoon vanilla extract

Combine all ingredients in bowl and beat until smooth and creamy. Yummy !

Recipe By Jonathan and Quinlan Brown Helen Brown (San Miguel Allende)

APPLES WITH CRUNCHY OATMEAL TOPPING

Ingredients:

3 apples, sliced thin
¾ Cup Oatmeal
¾ Cup Brown Sugar
½ Cup Butter
½ Cup Flour

Instructions:

Core apples

Peel, slice and place in greased round pan

Combine oatmeal, sugar and flour

Cut in butter (Melt, if you are in a hurry)
Sprinkle over apples

Bake at 350 for 35-40 minutes Serve warm (with cream or milk)

Note: A favorite childhood memory of Jonathan's

Recipe and Scripture by Cheri Long   (Austin, Texas)
1 Corinthians 13: 4-8 Love is patient, love is kind

With thanks to my late aunt and uncle, J.D. and John Dowdy, U.S. House of Representatives 3rd District, Texas. My aunt made this cake often, but the recipe is rare now.

RILEY´S TEXAS PECAN CAKE

Ingredients:

6 Unbeaten egg whites
1 pound light brown sugar
2 and 2/3 cups sifted all-purpose flour
½ teaspoon baking powder
3 cups broken pecans
1 teaspoon vanilla

Method:

Preheat the oven to 300F

Prepare two loaf pans or one bundt pan, buttering, dusting with flour

Whisk together egg whites and brown sugar, until they're well mixed.
Fold in blended dry ingredients, pecans and vanilla.

Pour into baking pan or bundt pan.

Bake for 1 hour and 15-20 minutes, until the cake pulls away from the sides of the pan. Baking time is about the same for loaf or bundt pans. The top will be cracked and crispy, the center sticky-moist.

Cool before cutting.

Easily frozen with several layers of aluminum foil-defrost in the wrapping.

Unusual to find such a fabulous old cake/confection recipe requiring so little prep time.

Recipe and scripture by: Sandra Sasser Pastora de Baptist Church in Mexico City with her husband Pastor Thomas Lynn Sasser for 24 years in Mexico.

Mathew 5:16 Let your light so shine before men, that they may see your good works, and glorify your Father which is in heaven.

WORLD'S BEST CHOCOLATE CHIP COOKIES

Preheat oven to 375 F/ 170 C

2 sticks softened unsalted butter
1/2 cup white sugar
1 1/2 cups Brown sugar
1 egg
1 tsp vanilla
2 cups flour (depends on altitude of where you live, in CDMX,1 add 1/4 cup more)
1/2 tsp salt
1/2 tsp. Soda
1/2 tsp. baking powder (for high altitude)
1 ½ cup chocolate chips
Cream butter and sugars together until smooth Add egg and vanilla mixing well together
Add flour, soda, salt , baking powder. Mix well. Add chocolate chips.
Drop by rounded spoonful on baking sheet/size depends on what you want. Bake for 15-20 minutes depending on your oven and altitude. Enjoy!

Recipe and scripture by: Karen Woodall (San Miguel Allende)

Gal. 3:29 If you belong to Christ, them you are Abraham's seed and heirs, according to the promise.

EASY COOKIES

2 tablespoons peanut butter (I use chunky)
18 oz. package butterscotch morsels
1 small package slice almonds
5-6 cups cornflake cereal

Melt peanut butter and morsels and stir until melted over low hear.

Pour mixture into bowl of cereal and nuts. Drop by spoonful on cookie sheet to make about 2 dozen and put into fridge for about 10 min.

They are then ready to eat and this is the easiest cookie ever to make and Yummy!

Receta y escritura de: Silvia Diaz (Cuidad de Mexico)

2 Corintios 9:9 -10 Comparten con libertad y dan con generosidad a los pobres. Sus buenas acciones serán recordadas para siempre. Pues es Dios quien provee la semilla al agricultor y luego el pan para comer. De la misma manera, el proveerá y aumentara los recursos de ustedes luego producirá un gran cosecha de generosidad en ustedes.

PAN DE AVENA
Hacer la preparación una noche antes

Ingredientes:

Molde de 20x20 cm
3 huevos enteros
1/2 taza de aceite
1/2 taza de azúcar
2 tazas de avena
1 taza de leche
1 1/2 cdita de canela
1 cdita vanilla

Procedimiento:
Se mezclan todos los ingredientes en un tazon hasta formar una mezcla homogénea Se vierte la mezcla a molde previamente engrasado y enharinado
Se refrigera toda la noche
Al día siguiente antes de hornear se espolvorea nuez picada, canela y azúcar moscabada al gusto
Se corta y se sirve clientito con crema batida o helada

Recipe by: Ann Diaz (France)

BUCKWHEAT CREPES

Makes about 18

3 cup freshly ground buckwheat flour
1 cup freshly ground spelt, kamut or whole wheat flour
4 cups buttermilk, kéfir or yogurt
4 cups buttermilk, kéfir or yoghurt
3 eggs , lightly beaten
1/2 teaspoon salt
About 1/2 cup melted butter

Soak flour in buttermilk, kéfir or yoghurt in warm place for 12 to 24 hours. Those with milk allergies may use 2 cups filtered with water plus 2 tablespoons whey lemon juice or vinegar in place of undiluted buttermilk, kéfir or yoghurt. Beat in eggs salt and 1/4 cup melted butter and thin with enough water to achieve the consistency of cream. Beat several min. with an electric beater and chill well. Heat a heavy skillet. Brush with melted butter and use a 1/4 -1/3 cup measure to ladle batter into pan. Tip pan to distribute batter. Turn after two min. and cook another min. Keep crepes warn in the oven while making the rest,brushing the pan with butter between each crepe. Fill with raw honey, apricot butter, sweet cheese topping grated raw cheese, ratatouille , crab filling or chicken supreme . Crepes may be made ahead of time and reheated.

Variation: Crispy Crepes

Spread crepes on a platter and leave in a 150 degree oven overnight. Crepes will dry out and become crispy. These are delicious with butter and raw honey.

Recipe and scripture by: Martha Beyer Pastora (California)

John 12: 14-15 I give you a new command: Love each other. You must love each other as I have loved you. All people will know that you are my followers if you love each other.

Martha and her husband Pastor Doug served as Pastors at the Union Church in Mexico city They were loved by so many and are missed until this day. Both are retired in California. Martha was taught to make this cobbler by her mother.

FRUIT COBBLER

1/2 c. margarine
1 c. flour
¾ c. sugar
2 tsp. baking powder
1/4 tsp salt
1 c. milk
1 c. fresh or canned fruit

Melt margarine in a 9 x13 inch baking dish Mix flour, sugar baking powder, salt and milk. Add to the margarine in the baking dish. Add the fruit and any juice. Sprinkle an additional 3/4 c sugar on top. Bake at 350 for 30-40 minutes . Enjoy!

Recipe by: Fabrizia Costa Photographer and Writer (Bath, UK)

BEST EVER CHOCOLATE LAVA CAKES!

Gluten-free and sugar-free – Only 5 ingredients!

3 very fresh large eggs
55 gr dark chocolate 85 percent cocoa
55 gr butter
1 and a half tbsp powdered sweetener, the best is xilitol
1 and a half tbsp almond flour

Turn on the oven to 180 C

Grease two or three small ramekins very well with butter.

In a microwave melt butter and chocolate in a bowl on low power.

Alternatively you can use a bowl placed over a saucepan with a Little hot water over low heat , stirring as it melts. Make sure the end result is well melted but lukewarm and not hot.

Leave to cool if necessary.

Whisk the eggs till very light and foamy with an electric whisk.

Add the sweetener and the almond flour and stir well. Add the melted chocolate/butter mix, making sure it´s not too warm. Stir well

Pour into the ramekins and bake for 9 min. They will be jiggly when they come out! Don't worry, they set as they cool. If you want them more fudgy, bake for a few extra min.(but I´d say…don't

Leave about 20 min. until lukewarm and serve. Enjoy!

You can also leave to cool and then cover with clingfilm and chill if you can´t eat it right away . Next day, run a knife along the Edge and flip onto a small dish. Microwave at 360 W (approx) for one min. Works perfectly. If you want to use sugar, the quantity is the same.

Receta de: Eugenia Trevino (Cuidad de Mexico)

BOMBA DE CHOCOLATE (Mariana)

Frase: "Tienes dos cartas: El No ya lo tienes, ve por el si"

Ingredientes:

170 gr. Mantequilla
60 gr. Azúcar
60 gr. Harina
3 huevos
3 yemas
170 gr. Chocolate semi amargo (puede ser alguna barra o las chispas de chocolate Hershey semiamargas)
1 bolsa de kisses o caja de chocolates lindt azúcar glass Modo de Hacerse

Se derrite el chocolate con la mantequilla en el microondas. Se bate el azúcar con 3 huevos y 3 yemas .

Se une al chocolate derretido con la mantequilla, se anade el harina cernida envolviendo. Se pone un poco en los moldes (engrasados con mucha mantequilla y harina para que no se peguen) En el centro se coloca una bola del chocolate lindt.

Luego se pone mas chocolate para cubrir la bola. Se precalienta el horno y se meten a 200 por 12 a 17 min. Tiene que salir inflados como soufflé. Checar que esten cocidos con un palillo. Se voltean directo al plato con helado al gusto. Se les espolvorea azúcar glass. Al partirlo caliente, sale el chocolate derretido mmmm…Si no se derrite, no pasa nada, saben igual de deliciosos.

Ahhhh ¡MUY IMPORTANTE!

Tienen que estar en el refrigerador por lo menos 6 horas antes de hornearlos. Es mas fácil se las preparas una noche antes.

Receta de : Marcela Echeverria Escuela CEPI (Cuidad de Mexico)

Disfruta de esta delicia!

CREMA DE LIMON CON FRUTAS

Ingredientes

1 lata de leche condensada helada
1 lata de leche evaporada helada
6 o 8 limones
Fruta al gusto (puede ser durazno, pina, fresa o platanos)

Preparacion

Se bate la leche evaporada hasta que levante se le va agregando la leche condensada poco a poco y se sigue batienda.

Hecho esto se la agrega el jugo de limon y se sigue batiendo hasta que espese la crema. Se le agrega la fruta y se pone en el refrigerador.

Se sirve con un poco de nuez picada encima. Rico

y refrescante postre!

Receta de: Ceci Gonzalez (Cuidad de Mexico)

GELATINA DE QUESO

Ingredientes:

1 lata leche clavel
1 lata leche Condensada
1 lata media Crema
1 pieza (grande) queso philadelphia y 3 sobres Grenetina Modo de Elaboracion

Disolver la grenetina en 3/4 de taza de agua, y meterla al microondas de 1 a 1:30, hasta que se disuelva perfectamente.

1. Se ponen todas las leches, el queso y la grenetina en la licuadura.

2. Se pone la mezcla en un molde y se refrigera hasta que cuaje.

Receta y escritura de: Frida Maurano es estudiante de Gastronoma (Cuidad de Mexico)

Galatas 5:22-26 Mas el fruto del espíritu es amor, gozo, paz , paciencia, benignidad, bondad, fe , mansedumbre, templanza, contra tales cosas no hay ley. Pero los que son de Vristo han crucificado la carne on sus pasiones y deseos. Si vivimos por el Espiritu, andemos tambien por el Espiritu. No nos hagamos vangloriosos, ,irritándonos unos a otros, envidiandonos nunos a otros.

EL PAY DE CALABAZA (Origen)

El pumpkin pie es común en las mesas de los americanos en la época de otoño ya que un ingrediente muy utilizado en la época es la calabaza de Castilla de Mesoamericanos; esta receta la fue realizando y perfeccionando el Chef Frances Pierre en 1651 pero a pesar de gran intento, lo ingleses tomaron dicha receta y comenzaron a trabajar en ella mas a fondo. En 1796 la receta se volvió muy famosa en America.

Ingredientes:

Para la base
2 tazas de harina
1 taza de mantequilla
1 huevo
2 cuchaaradas de azúcar
1 pizcar de sal
Para el relleno
2 tazas de pulpa de calabaza de Castilla o calabaza mantequilla cocida
3 huevos
1 yema
1 taza de crema para batir
1 cucharadita de canela
1/2 cucharadita de clavo molido
1/2 cucharadita de nuez moscada
1/2 cucharadita de cardamomo
1/2 cucharadita de piel de limon
1/2 cucharadita de jengibre en polvo Para crema
2 tazas de crema para batir
1 cucharadita de cardamomo

Procedimiento:

Es una receta para aprox. 6 rebanadas, tiempo de preparación 1 hr. Tiempo de coccion 30 min. Precalenta el horno a 180 C

Para hacer la base

1) Mezclar harina cernida con azúcar y sal.

2) Agregar la mantequilla en cubos, integrar poco a poco hasta que quede una textura arenosa. Hacer una fuente: Juntar la mezcla y dejar un hoyo en el medio (algo asi como un volcán)

3) Agregar vanilla y huevo hacer homogeneo. Poco a poco los ingredientes se empezaran a unir. La idea es amasarla lo menos posible para que no se haga elástica y pierda forma en el horno. Estara lista cuando, al presionar la contra la mesa no haya grumos de mantequilla

4) Empacar en plástico o egapack y reservar en el refrigerador durante 40 min. Esto bajara la temperatura de la mantequilla y terminara de darle consistencia a la masa.

5) En un rejilla o charola, poner un aro para pay o molde. Sacar la masa del refrigerador, extender con un rodillo y con mucho cuidado, ponerla sobre el molde.

6) La masa debe quedar pegada y pareja. Con un tenedor, hacer pequeños orificios en la base; esto va a servir para que no pierda forma al hornear. Con la yema de los dedos, levantar un poco los bordes del molde, como en forma de pellizco, para hacer la decoración de la orilla. Refrigerar o congelar.

Para hacer el relleno

Con una cuchara, despulpar la calabaza. Es muy importante quitar todas las fibras y semillas para que el relleno tenga un textura mas cremosa.

1. En un sarten con poca mantequilla, poner la calabaza rebanada para sellarla. Esto va a prevenir que la calabaza se hidrate de mas y el relleno quede muy liquido. Cuando empiece a tomar color y a ablandarse, retirar del fuego.

2. Cocer la calabaza en agua o leche. Secar muy bien y partir en cubos.

3. En un bowl, mezclar la calabaza con el huevo y la yema hasta que se haga homogeneo. Se puede hacer con un batidor de globo. La idea es que no queden grumos de la calabaza.

4. Agregar las especias.

5. Agregar la crema hasta que quede homogeneo. Verter la mezcla en la base y hornear por 30 min.

Para el montaje

1. Calenta un poco la crema y sin que hierva, agregar un chucharadita de cardamomo. Mezclar y enfriar.
2. Una vez teniendo la crema completamente fría, montarla en una batidora de globo.
3. Una vez cocido el pay, refrigerar.
4. Decorar con la crema montada.

Conclusion: Esta receta me gusta mucho realmente, se me hace una receta muy completa pero la reposteria es asi,completa y delicada como esta receta, tienes que aprender a distinguir cada sabor de cada especie que agregas, reposteria es de paciencia y de leer todo con detenimiento, es alegría y concentración. Asi esta receta me recuerda al versículo que lei hace poco, yo soy nueva en el cristianismo y me considero afortunada de a ver empezado este camino con Dios, el dia tras dia me cuida y me apoya, es el apoyo que yo necesitaba en mi vida que será para sie

Recipe and scripture by: Fran Gamboa (Mexico city)

Romans 12:12 Be joyful in hope, patient in affliction, faithful (or constant) in prayer.

PEANUT BUTTER COOKIES

Ingredients:

1 cup of peanut butter
1 cup of sugar
1 egg

Blend together

Use a spoon to drop dough onto baking sheet and the take fork to smash each lump one down crossing the tines.

This gives the typical peanut butter cookie look

Bake at 170 C until done – About 7-8 minutes

It's very simple but very yummy. Small children can do it with a little help from adults.

Receta de Maria Del Socorro Maldonado Hdez. Casa Abierta al Tiempo 54834000 ext. 1772 (Cuidad de Mexico)

PASTEL DE CHOCOLATE

Ingredientes:

2 tazas de harina de trigo, taza y media de azúcar, una y media mantequilla Gloria de 90 gms.,3/4 de taza de coco Hersey, 4 huevos a temperatura ambiente, 3/4 de taza de leche, 2 cucharaditas de royal, una cucharadita de extracto de vainilla y una pizca de sal.

Preparacion:

Se cierne la harina, la cocoa, el royal y la pizca de sal y todo eso se incorpora bien, se deja por separado. Se derrite la mantequilla en el bol de cristal 40 segundos en el horno de microondas y se le incorporal la leche, huevos, azúcar y la vainilla. S mezcla todo con la batidora por espacio de 3 a 4 min., se va incorporando la harina de poco en poco con los ingredientes ya integrados (cocoa, royal, sal) a que

se incorporen muy bien y se sigue batiendo hasta considerar que ya esta listo para vaciarlo al monde previamente engrasado.

El horno ya debe de estar caliente a temperatura 200 grados. Se mete el molde y se baja la temperatura a 160 grados por espacio de 40 min. O considerar que ya esta listo.

Se bañar con chocolate amargo derretido en baño maría.

Receta de: Olivia Martinez (San Miguel Allende)

PASTEL DE CHOCOLATE

Ingredientes:

100 gr. Nuez
175 Gr. Chocolate
1 late de leche condensada
5 huevos

Preparacion

Se licuan todos los ingredientes y se vacian en un molde previamente engrasado,se hornea a 180 por 30 min. Espolvorear azúcar glass para decorar.

Recipe: Virginia L Harford (Photographer) (San Miguel Allende)

CHOCOLATE AVOCADO TRUFFLES

Ingredients

3/4 cup unsweetened dark chocolate
1 avocado, pitted and skinned
teaspoon chocolate-flavored liquid Stevia
1/2 teaspoon vanilla extract
Pinch of ground cinnamon Pinch of sea salt
1/2 teaspoons raw cacao powder, for coating

Instructions:

Step 1 Place a heat – safe glass bowl inside a medium saucepan filled with 1 inch of water over low heat. Place the chocolate in the bowl and allow to slowly melt, stirring occasionally.

Step 2 In a separate bowl, mash the avocado. When the chocolate has fully melted, remove from the heat and transfer it to the bowl containing the mashed avocado. Stir them together, then add the Stevia, vanilla extract, cinnamon, and salt. Stir until fully combined and free of clumps. Refrigerate for 30 minutes, or until cooled and hardened.

Step 3 Scoop the mixture into 10 to 12 equal-sized balls and roll them until they are smooth.

Step 4 Place the cacao powder in a shallow bowl. Roll each ball in the cacao powder and serve immediately. Store any leftover truffles in an airtight container in the refrigerator for up to a week.

Recipe and scripture by: Sandra Orellana Writer (San Miguel Allende)

CAPIROTADA

Ingredients:

Half dozen toasted buttered bread (I use bimbo bread)
Nuts (chopped)
Peanuts Raisins
Cheese (Mozzarella)
Cinnamon
Pilosiyo (Brown sugar)

Layer the bread and top mix ingredients Put it in the oven for 30 min.
Sprinkle confetti candy over it for decoration Serve hot or cold

Recipe and scripture by: Daina Jasmine Venture (San Miguel Allende)

TIRAMISU

Serves 8

250 gr. Mascarpone (Galbani or Belgioioso or Remo's)
A pack of Savoiardi (Ladies Fingers)
Cocoa powder or dark chocolate Sugar
Pinch of salt Coffee

First of all make, some coffee (In whatever way you like it and you can use decaf if you prefer) let it cool off at room temperature or in the fridge if you don't have time to wait.

Meanwhile separate the yolk from the white of the eggs into two bowls, mount the White with the aid o fan electric whip with a pinch of salt until it's firm and thick.

On the other bowl mount the yolks with sugar (apx ac cup) until creamy and whitened, add the 250 gr Mascarpone cream in the bowl and mix well until it´s a soft cream, if you like you can add any liquor or brandy, rum, or coffee liquor. Then add the mounted white and incorporate it gently.

Soak ladies finger in the cold coffee, be careful not to soak them too long as they melt easily. Just a quick dip in the coffee would do.

Set the soaked ladies fingers into a recipient big enough to hold the Tiramisu. Cover them with the Mascarpone and eggs cream, make another layer of ladiesfingers on top and another one of cream then pour the cocoa powder with the help of a sieve or strainer and if you like you can also finish with some dark chocolate grated on top. Put in the fridge for at least 2 hours.

Receta de : Marcela Jimenez Cortes (Cuidad de Mexico)

GELATINA DE CAJETA

Ingredientes:

litros de leche
1/2 lt. De cajeta
sobres de gelatina sin sabor
1/2 taza de nuez picada
sobre
tazas de agua

Calentar la leche a que hierva. Mientras disolver la gelatina en 1/4 taza de agua tibia. Agregar la gelatina y la cajeta a la leche sin dejar de mover

Poner la nuez en el fondo del molde

Al hervir la leche poner en el molde y dejar enfriar. Luego refrigerar hasta que haya cuajado. Desmoldar y si gusta adornar con crema chantilly.

Recommendation if your in the áreas in San Miguel Allende

Recta y escritura de: Lic Enfermeria y Tanatologa Jaqueline Salgado 415 125 0399 (San Miguel Allende)

Filipenses 4:13 Todo lo puedo en Cristo que me fortalece

PAY DE LIMON

Ingredientes:

1 lata de lechera
1 lata de leche condensada
Jugo de 6 limones
2 paquetes de galletas marias Se pone en licuadora
Hecha la mezcla se coloca en un refractario y se acomodan las galletas, se refrigera por 2 horas y listo.

Receta de: Coco (San Miguel Allende)

MOUSE DE FRESA

Ingredientes:

1 taza de fresas
1 taze de yogurt natural
1 gelatina sabor fresa
Disuelta en 1 tasa de agua caliente y se deja en friar.

Se coloca todo en la licuadora se vacia en un molde y se refigera por una hora o hasta que toe textura de mouse.

Se puede hacer con crema acida pero con yogurt queda mas ligero.

Receta de: Genoveva Monterrubio (Cuidad de Mexico)

STRUDEL DER MANZANA

Ingredientes

1kg de pasta de hojaldre
2kg de manzana starkin roja
Nueces
Pasas
Manera de hacerse

Pelar manzanas en trozos chicos. Cocer sin agua con 1 clavo, 1 raja de canela, 1 limon exprimido y azúcar al gusto. Taparlo y que no quede bien cocido con los trozos de manzana enteros, dejarlo enfriar.

Estrirar la pasta hojaldrada que quede delgada.

Agregar un poquito de pan molido en las manzanas para absorber el jugo, una vez que este sin jugo, agregar pasas y nueces

Colocar la mezcla de la manzana con pasas y nueces sobre la pasta extendida y en rollar.

Batir en un molde un huevo separando las claras y la yema

Sellar con las claras las orillas del rollo ya envuelto.

Agregar donde esta la yema batida, azúcar y canela con una coladera. Untar sobre el rollo envuelto

Colocar en un molde y hornear con temperatura no muy fuerte por espacio de 1 hr.

Receta de: Susana Curiel Garcia   Biologa   (Cuidad de Mexico)

Ingredientes:

3/4 Taza Azucar refinada, para el caramelo
1 Lata leche condensada
1 Lata leche Evaporada
6 Piezas Huevo
1 cucharada esencia de vainilla

Instrucciones:

Vierte el azúcar en una flanera y calienta a fuego meido para que se forme el caramelo; ladea con cudiado el molde para cubrir la superficie y las paredes.

Licuar la leche condensada con a leche evaporada, los huevos y la esencia de vainilla. Vierte la preparación en la flanera y tapa con papel aluminio sellando las orillas. Coloca en una olla de presión y cocina a baño Maria por 30 min. a partir de que empiece a sonar la válvula.

Retirar del fuego y deja enfriar por completo; desmolda y sirve.

Consejo culinario: Para saber si el flan esta cocido, introduce la punta de un cuchillo; si sale limpia el flan esta listo.

Recipes and scripture by: DD Spivey (Oak Park)

MICAH 6:8 He has shown you, O mortal, what is good. Amd what does the Lord require of you? To act justly (A) and tol ove mercy and to walk humbly [a] (B) with your God. (C)

Ingredientes:

  1 stick margarine
  1 cup Graham cracker crumbs
  1 pkg. Chocolate chips
  1 can coconut
  1 cup pecans chopped
  1 can Eagle Brand condensed milk

Melt margarine in 9 x 13 pan over that pour Graham cracker crumbs, over that chocolate chips, over that coconut, over that pecans, over that Eagle Brand milk. Bake 300 degrees for 40 min.

Cool cut into squares.

Recipe and scripture by: DD Spivey (Oak Park)

Micah 6:8 He has shown you, O mortal, what is good. And what does the Lord require of you? To act justly (A) and to love mercy and to walk humbly [a] (B) with your God. (C)

DIRT CAKE

Ingredientes:

1 4 oz cream cheese
1 3/4 cups milk
1 4 oz cool whip
1 3 oz French vanilla pudding
1/2 cup confectioners sugar
1/2 cup butter
1 sm to med flower pot

In a bowl, mix confectioners sugar, butter and cream cheese. Mix till creamy. In a separate bowl, mix milk, pudding mix and cool whip till blended. Combine the 2 bowls of ingredients together. You'll need to put wax paper, aluminum foil or something to cover hole in the flower pot. Place a layer of Oreos in the flower pot, then a layer of mixture. Continue alternating layer, making sure to finish with Oreos.

After the pot is full, add fresh or silk flowers for decoration. Gummy worms make a great addition.

Notes:

Notes:

Extra Fun Recipes

Recipe by: Ginger Juhl

HOT WING DIP

Ingredients:

2 cups shredded cooked chicken
1 package (8 ounces) cream cheese, softened
1 1/2 cup Frank′s Red Hot pepper sauce
1/2 cup ranch dressing
1/2 cup blue cheese crumbles

DIRECTIONS:

1 PREHEAT oven to 350 degrees F. Mix all ingredients in a large bowl. Spoon into shallow 1-quart baking dish.

2 BAKE 20 minutes or until mixture is heated through; stir. Sprinkle with green onions, if desired, and serve with sliced French bread, chips, crackers and/ or cut up veggies.

Receta de : MaEsther Tapia Rosales (Tenacingo)

LIMONADA CON HIERBABUENA

4 porciones Ingredientes:
2 limones verdes (sin semilla)
Azucar la necesaria
8 ramitas de hierbabuena 1 litro de agua
Cubitos de hielo

Preparacion:
Pelar los limones (si se desea) cortarlos en trozos pequeños y licuar junto con el azúcar y la hierba buena con una taza de agua, color en una jarra y volver a hacer el procedimiento de molido y colado una vez mas. Colocarle los hielos y listo. Adorar el vaso con una rodaja de limon y una hoja de hierbabuena. Puedes usar menta pero unas dos ramitas. Esta limonada me encanta. Mi mama nos la hacea y es muy saludable y refrescante.

Recipe by Mary Jane Miller (San Miguel de Allende)

HOW TO STORE AND HEAT UP A TORTILLA PROPERLY

Tortillas are a mainstay of any Mexico kitchen. Mothers sit by the stove, heating them one at a time and hand them out as needed. In this era, the moms send their kids to the tortillería for a kilo of warm or cold tortillas in paper wrapping. If you leave them on the counter they curl and get stiff and dried out. We must properly store tortillas.

Separate the out to cool and wrap the in a cloth and then in a plastic bag to store in the fridge. How many times have you opened the plastic bag and found your tortilla molding or with a kind of cobweb happening? This is because they were stored poorly: put into a plastic bag when they were too hot.

Tortillas have two sides. A back and a front: The back is flat, thicker and the 'stomach or panza' is papery thin. When you heat a tortilla, always heat the back first, for two or three minutes. When the papery side expands, you flip the tortilla over and heat for a 30 seconds. Do Not flip them over and over. A burnt tortilla is more tasty than a dry cold one. Wrap them in a clean kitchen cloth 'servieta' to serve. Those pretty reed baskets with a lid make a lovely presentation.

GREEN SALSA

Ingredients:

2 - 5 green chiles, de-seeded
3 - 6 green tomatillos Cilantro
Salt
One clove garlic A bit of onion

Boil with a tiny bit of water until tender and blend in the blender
OR

Toast on a skillet till tender and then blend in the blender

Receta de: Nadia Barrera Montes 915 153 8892

TORTILLAS DE HARINA (Hecho en Casa)

980 gr. De harina
80 gr. De aceite vegetal
250 gr. De agua
Una cucharachita de Royal
Una pizca de sal

Recipe by: Sandra Orellana Writer (San Miguel Allende)

Green Juice " Juego Verde " at home

Ingredients:

Cucumber

Parsley

Orange

Celery Green

Apple

Spinach

Preparation:

Blend all ingredients in a high power blender

Notes:

Chef Sebastian Galvez Conde

Sebastian delights the senses with elegant ambiance, gracious service and highly pleasing menú in Casa Diamante Hotel Boutique Restaurant Chilcuague.

The name of the restaurant is named from a root called Chilcuague from Sierra Gorda. This root gives a tingling effect in the mouth as the food touches the tongue, it comes into contact with the sensory papillae and it gives a stronger delightful flavor when you taste the food.

PECHUA CASA DIAMANTE: Exclusive Dish (Recipe in Spanish)

La pechuga casa diamante es un platillo de pollo relleno de queso, tocino y vegetales envuelto en tocino acompañado de pure de amote, salsa de guajillo y morita y ensalada balsámica.

La ensalada.

Ingredientes:

Lechuga italiana 2 hojas
Lechuga sangria 2 hojas
Lechuga achicoria 2 hojas
Acelga 2 hojas
Arugula 8 hojas
Jitomate Cherry orgánico 8 pza.
Fresa 4 pza.
Espinaca baby 8 hojas
Arandano deshidratado 20 gr.
Nuez garapiñada 35 gr.
Queso de cabra 60 gr.
Aceite de oliva 80 ml.
Vinagre balsamico añejo 35 ml.
Sal de mar c/ s
Pimienta negra c/s

Preparacion:

Lavar y desinfectar todos los vegetales con abundante agua, y el desinfectante.

Cortar el jitomate Cherry por mitades, cortar la fresa en cuartos, desmoronar el queso y romper la nuez garapiñada

En un bowl mezclar las lechugas y hojas verdes con el jitomate, la fresa, el arandano, la nuez, el queso de cabra y sazonar ligeramente con sal y pimienta.

Mezclar el aceite de oliva y el vinagre balsamico, agitar bien.

Reservar.

Para el pure de camote:

Ingredientes:

Camote amarillo 500 gr.
Sal de mar c/s
Pimienta negra molida. c/s
Mantequilla 70 gr.
Canela molida 4 gr.
Miel de agave 25 ml

Preparacion:

1. Limpiar muy bien el camote con agua y una fibra.
2. Hervir el camote hasta que este completamente suave y pase un cuchillo sin problemas.
3. Quitar la cascara del camote, y sacar el relleno con una cuchara, Aplastar hasta consistencia de pure, de preferencia pasar por un tamizador para que sea muy fino.
4. En un sarten poner la mantequilla y calentar, agregar el pure de camote, y sazonar
5. El sabor tiene que ser ligeramente agridulce, reservar.

Para la salsa:

Ingredientes:

chile morita 2 pza.
Chile guajillo 5 pza.
Cebolla 50 gr.
Ajo 10 gr.
Sal de mar c/s

Preparacion:

1. Cortar y quita a parte verde del poro, retirar la ultima capa.
2. Cortar en julianas super finas las capas blancas del poro, freir hasta que tomen un color paja, escurrir y reservar.

Para la pechuga:

Relleno damante:

Ingredientes:

Queso crema 150 gr.
Queso de cabra 150 gr.
Tocino 150 gr.
Champiñon 4 pza
Cebolla blanca 100 gr
Ajo 10 gr
Chile pblano 50 gr
Perejil 3 gr Pimienta negra c/s
Sal de mar c/c

Preparacion:

1. Picar finamente el tocino, la cebolla, el ajo, el chile poblano (sin semillas), el champiñón y el perejil.

2. Sofreír el tocino en una sarten, agregar cebolla, chile y ajo, cuando este bien sofrito agregar el champiñón, retirar del fuego y agregar ambos quesos, mezclar y sazonar con la pimienta negra, sal de mar y perejil.
3. Reservar.

Para la pechuga:

Ingredientes:

Milanesa de pechuga de pollo 4 pza. de 120 gr aprox.
Tocino en laja delgada 250 gr
Espinaca 8 hojas
Sal de mar c/s
Pimienta negra c/s
Aceite vegetal 20 ml
Relleno 400 gr

Preparacion:

1. Salpimentar la pechuga, poner una cama de espinaca y el relleno, envolver en forma de rollo y cubrir con el tocino como si fuera vendaje.

2. En un sarten poner un poco de aceite y sofreír la pechuga hasta dorar el tocino por todas partes girando poco a poco la pechuga.
3. Cortar por la mitad y reservar para el montaje. Montaje de plato:
En un plato regla largo poner de un lado la ensalada de mixta y bañar con vinagreta. El pure de camote va en el otro lado del plato, poner la pechuga partida a la mitad sobre el, bañar con salsa de guajillo y morita, poner poro frito y decorar con brotes de temporada.

Interview with Chef Sebastian:

What do you enjoy about being a Chef?
What I like the most about being a chef is surprising the diner, and seeing their positive reaction to the dishes, seeing how them make them happy.

What motivates you to do your best on the job?
What motivates me is to become an important exhibitor of Mexican gastronomy in the world, and to teach how amazing Mexico is.

Who is a Chef you admire and why?
One of the chefs I most admire is Francis Mallmann, I admire him because he is a great lover of fire, and an authentic person without fear of receiving criticism for his dishes, cooking or his way of being.

How is your food hygiene and safety while working?
It is important to emphasize that hygiene measures have always been of the greatest importance, to thoroughly clean the areas of use, disinfect fruits and vegetables, be careful not to break food temperature chains, correct food conservation, use of mouth covers and gloves, adequate and continuous hand washing, as well as adequate and organic pest control.

Why do you want to work as a Chef at this restaurant?
Because it is a Mexican restaurant, where I can create and innovate, because I love the staff and because I have been in love with the Project for several years.

Can you tell me about a time when you've had a dish returned to the kitchen?
They returned a plate to me because the beef cut did not have the proper term, and it is a very sad feeling but it is for the better, so the dish is changed, a proper apology is made and we learn from our mistakes.

How do you imagine a typical day in work?
Make purchases in the market, select the freshest products, arrive at the restaurant and start making mise en plase, customers arrive and the service begins, deep cleaning is done, you see what you have to buy and do for the next day.

What do you look for when you hire Chefs?
Good attitude and desire to learn and improve, likewise open mind and desire to join the team.

Where do you see yourself in five year's time?
With the Casa Diamante Project consolidated in Mexico and with a Chilcuague restaurant abroad.

Do you have a sense of humor?
I like to joke, laugh and have fun while I work, and when talking to my clients I like to be very entertaining and have good vibes.

Notes:

Thank you to the following individuals and businesses for their support Show your book to receive a discount from:

Antaño Restaurante
Ancha de San Antonio # 4 tel: 415 150 1321 (San Miguel Allende)

Casa Diamante Hotel Boutique
Viñedos Azteca (Ezequiel Montes Queretaro Mexico)

Restaurante Chilcuague

El Rincosito Resturante: tradicional comida Manuel (415 216 05 22) San Miguel Allende

Lum Inmobiliaria
Karin Olguin   5548364803 Broker Inmobiliario Cuidad de Mexico

Liverpool Restaurante (San Miguel Allende)

Pizzaretys
Calle: San Antonio # 373 Col: San Pedro de los Pinos 5556156200 hasta 05 Dueño Eduardo Angeles Garcia (Cuidad de Mexico)

Lourdes Bucio 3318508623 Un Estudio de experimentación textil Manejo de Maquina de Coser, Patch work , Bordado. (San Miguel Allende)

Ario Quimica SA de CV (Pintura)
Lidia Maturano   5555081472 (Cuidad de Mexico)

Estetoclinica
Maria Ofelia   # 1522935   Viridiana Hernandez Diaz

Flor's Cafe
Plaza Brisas # 415 1212135

Koe Sma Boutique de Carnes
5535393851 # 4151195147   La Lejona (cercas de Mega)

Lacteos Chely   (Quesos Chely)
Carretera SMA Dr. Mora Km 31 415 151 0303 Taña Vargas

Clases particulares de Ingles Nadia Barrera Montes
Capacitacion de ventas en idioma # 915 153 8892

Manzanita Store: Servicio de reparación de computadoras
Plaza Brisas Local 14 # 415 121 6186 (San Miguel)

Irma Obregon Pintora
www.irmaobregon.com.mx

El Fogon Taqueria Restaurant
El Paso TX 301 Paisano Drive

Tripping Mexico – Luxury Vacations Rentals
FB: Tripping Mexico
IG: @trippingmexico.com WhatsApp 5537339973

D. T E I Stay Simple Handmade (purses)
Tienda.dtei@gmail.com

Enamora – Te Desayunos
Plaza La Luciérnaga (San Miguel Allende) 415 120 51 90

Fumigaicon y Cafeteria
Sirael Ramirez Rubio   415 1497988

Eric Fash – Computer / Phone Consulting & Training
+1 440 527 1292
ericfash@gmail.com

Casa Lotería
José de la Amistad

Notes:

Notes:

Bookcover Recipes

Book cover recipe: Beef Tenderloin with red wine mushroom sauce

A 3lb. Beef tenderloin, trimmed

1 ½ teaspoons salt

3/4 teaspoon freshly ground pepper

3 teaspoons extra virgin olive oil , 2 large shallots, minced , 12 oz crimini mushrooms, cleaned and sliced
¾ cup red wine (Cabernet Sauvignon) 1 1/2 cups beef broth, 3 tablespoons butter

1) Preheat oven to 400 F . Prepare a large rimmed baking sheet or a rack in a pan with cooking oil.

2) Tie Kitchen string (cotton) around the beef in 4 places. Rub the meat with 1 teaspoon of salt and 1/2 pepper.

3) Heat 1 teaspoon olive oil in large frying pan over medium-heat. Add beef and brown on all sides for a total of 6-8 minutes. Transfer to the prepared pan.

4) Roast the beef until thermometer inserted in the thickest part reaches 140 F for medium-rare , about 35 minutes. Let rest with aluminum foil tented over it for 10 minutes before slicing.

5) Meanwhile, heat 2 teaspoons of olive oil in the same frying pan over medium-high heat. Add shallots and cook for 30 seconds. Stir in sliced mushrooms, 1/2 teaspoon salt, 1/4 teaspoon pepper. Cook stirring occasionally and scraping up any browned bits, until mushrooms are slightly browned , about 3-5 minutes. Pour in wine, bring to a boil and cook until liquid has reduced by a third, about 3-5 minutes. Turn off heat and swirl in butter until melted.

6) Removing string and slice beef to desired thickness .
Serve with mushroom sauce.

Book cover Recipe: Scalloped Potatoes

3 lbs potatoes, peeled and sliced very thinly 2 cloves garlic, minced
6 tablespoons unsalted butter cut into small pieces 3 cups heavy cream
Salt and pepper

1)	Preheat oven to 325 F. Rub a 9x13 glass baking dish with butter. Arrange half the potatoes nicely layered and dot with half the butter, half the garlic, salt and pepper. Repeat with the rest of the potatoes, garlic, butter, salt and peeper. Pour the heavy cream on top and spread evenly.

2)	Bake for 1 hour and 20 minutes until potatoes are tender and bubling. Increase oven temperatura to 400 and continue baking about 10 minutes more until top is slightly browned. Let stand covered with aluminum foil for 15 minutes before sefvinng.

Book cover Recipe: Rosemary Garlic Bread

1 1/2 teaspoons active dry yeast
1 cup warm water
2teaspoons sugar
2 teaspoons saltr
1 tablespoon dried Rosemary
1/4 teaspoon freshly ground black pepper
1/2 teaspoon dried oregano
1 head of roasted garlic
Extra olive oil for spreading on top Coarse sea salt
Clean water in a spray bottle

1) In a large bowl, sprinkle yeast in 1 cup of warm water. Mix in the sugar and salt. Let sit for 10 minutes until it foams. Add in olive oil. Add flour and knead for 10 minutes . Add rosemary, pepper and oregano. Knead for another 5 minutes. Gently knead in roasted, peeled garlic by hand, about 1 minute.

2) Place dough ball in a well oiled bowl turning the dough a few times so it's covered with oil. Tightly cover bowl with plastic wrap. Place in a warm área until dough has doubled in size , about 1 hour . If it's cold day it may take up to 2 hours.

3) After dough has doubled. Punch it down and shape i tinto a round loaf.With a sharp knife score a criss cross ontop. Place onto a Grease baking sheet. Cover loaf with a large mixing bowl inverted over it. Let rise until doubled again, about 1 hour.

4) After dough has doubled, remove bowl, brush with olive oil and sprinkle with coarse salt and more rosemarey. Bake in a pre-heated oven set at 375 F for 25- 30 minutes, spraying with water a couple of times during baking. Turn up oven temperatura to 425F spray loaf with water again an bake until golden, being careful not to over bake. 5) Serve with olive oil and balsamic vinegar for dipping.

A meal with a scripture invites you to take time to pray and connect with God. Cooking is to make a feast with your family and friends sharing their favorite recipes.

Sandra Orellana is a retired teacher, author of *The Arch of Surprises*, *Liz's Key of Life*, Children's book *Leo's Bliss: The Sky*. Short Stories published and her devotional book: *One on One It´s Personal* soon to be published. Writer of the month. Her passions are tennis, cooking, people, and reaching out to the most in need. She loves to encourage young adults to read the Bible. She lives in San Miguel Allende. She can be found on Twitter, Facebook, and her blog.